string bean

carl miller daniels

BareBackPress

This is a work of fiction. The characters, incidents, and dialogue are the products of the author's imagination and are not to be construed as real. Any resemblance to actual events or person, living or dead, is entirely coincidental.

BareBackPress
Hamilton, Ontario, Canada
For information visit www.barebackpress.com
Cover layout by P. Jelen
Cover photography by Carl Miller Daniels

No part of this can be used or reproduced in any manner whatsoever without written permission, except in the case of brief quotations embodied in critical articles and reviews. For information address BareBackPress.

COPYRIGHT © 2018 Carl Miller Daniels
All RIGHTS RESERVED
ISBN-13: 978-1926449180
ISBN-10: 1926449185

POEMS

string bean - 1
not in my english class you don't - 2
a time like no other - 5
flamingo waltz - 7
life lessons - 9
muddy toes - 10
reverence for falling stars - 12
i think he said his name was "lucky" - 13
who is god - 15
idealist - 16
the erasmusic of buttered lunacy - 19
ullage - 21
blessed be - 23
the sweet smell of decay - 26
the dignity of cloth napkins - 33
missed opportunities - 34
creosote pineapple - 36
both of us 20 years old, him & me - 37
taxonomy - 43
alarmist - 45
prettier - 47
peace peace peace - 48
attitude - 49
regrets only - 52
that word - 53
got time for a quickie - 55
horsepower and the art of mustang maintenance - 56
oligocene chastity - 58
the scarcity of ripe peaches - 60
wahoo! - 61
do you say "supper" or "dinner"? - 62

just babbling away again,
enjoying the heck out of cliches, life, everything - 64
not really theft - 66
pollen lampshades - 67
sheaths and quivers - 68
motherfuck - 70
picking daisies - 72
yes Yes YES - 75
zephyrs - 77
self portrait, sorting socks - 78
the sensation of really thick breadmold - 79
trans-atlantic determination - 80
open-hearth policy - 82
rope and tiger - 83
prurient salsa - 86
hairy knuckles - 88
big-boned - 90
green green green - 92
do not leave chewing gum in water fountain - 94
bloom - 95
just flirting - 96
bye - 97
cheap shot - 99
always look twice before crossing the street - 101
slower, yes, much more slowly than that - 103
good B.J. (conceptually speaking) - 104
don't put turnips in your pockets - 107
the sidewalk - 109
prick - 111
sparklers on the 4th of july - 114
open window - 116
combo - 118
trouser trout - 120

individual rights in the time of crisis - 122
dinner time yet - 123
rounds - 125
flavor - 126
patterns on the landscape of dreams - 127
peaches and pears - 129
smackers and crackers - 130
twice that many - 131
too too - 133
spread 'em - 134
poe, hawthorne, and melville -- sir! - 135
cranberry juice spritzer with twist of vodka pete, please - 137
luna lunar lunatic - 138
generic cough syrup - 140
how platonic - 142
the neophytes - 145
lentils - 146
just the thumbs - 147
slurp - 149
liniment, the panacea of earthly delights - 151
grandson effectiveness -153
marigold jelly - 154
sandpaper quilts - 156
greco-roman wrestling - 158

for Jon

aka "the sweetest man in the world"

"Cheese is milk's leap toward immortality."
～ Clifton Fadiman

string bean
Carl Miller Daniels

string bean

i was secretly plotting my own suicide
when fate intervened, and i got
sent to a mental hospital for 3 months.
i emerged from the mental hospital
only half-crazy. no longer suicidal,
but kinda half wild, half terrified,
my thoughts of an
undefined and
gauzily amorphous
nature. i was just 18.
now,
i'm 63, long ago met
the man i love, and have been
living with him
for over 30 years.
we're good together.
i feel lucky.
now, when
i think back about
a lot of things in my life,
i feel kinda nostalgic
mellow, and
puzzled, actually,
by the apparent happenstance of
it all. who knew things would
turn out okay?
i'm looking out the window at
this very moment. it's october.
autumn leaves in all those
pretty autumn colors.
yep,
i'm almost 64 now,
and
just kinda
amazed.

not in my english class you don't

big-eyed sexy teenage boy who has
plans to
be a biologist
inhales.
the gray-green goop smells
musty, musky, earthy. he's
here in the woods,
naked, all alone,
and he didn't really mean to
get distracted by this
gray-green musky goop.
mainly he's here because he
just wants to
jerk off, all alone out here in
the woods. he feels sexy out
here, naked, in the sunshine,
woodsy leafy smells, little birds singing,
insects clicking and clacking away.
but now, his attention keeps
going back to that
gray-green goop growing on
top of a pile of dry brown leaves.
what the heck is that goop anyway?
a slime mold of some kind?
a lichen? a fungus? some
kind of algae maybe?
down on his hands
and knees, sticking the
tip of his nose
practically right
in it,
the big-eyed sexy teenage boy
with plans to be a
biologist
suddenly feels like sticking some
of it, well, sticking some of
it back THERE. you know, back
THERE. so he stares at

the stuff some more.
gray-green goop, kinda slimy
in texture. gooey. icky, kinda repulsive,
and yet. and yet...
his little butt is in the air.
his legs are kinda spread apart.
there's a gentle breeze. it's cool,
yet warm, and it's blowing on
him, blowing gentle sweet sexy
right on the
pink rim of his, well, right on
the rim of tight little
asshole. the breeze feels
cool and tingly, and thoughts
are racing sparkly hot inside
the sloshy wet pinkness of
his almost-a-biologist's
brain. and so now,
the big-eyed sexy teenage boy
with plans to be a biologist
pinches off a
little blob of the gray-green goop
between his thumb and index finger.
squishes it up some more.
reaches back to his asshole,
applies just a little bit to the rim. just
a little bit. just a sample.
so moist. so cool. so well,
maybe push a little of it
right on inside. right on in, just
a little bit, he's
down on his hands and knees
in the forest, his butt is in the air,
his tight little asshole is pink and
ready for the procedure,
big-eyed sexy teenage boy who
wants to be a biologist
performs the
experiment, plans to keep it secret,
just better off that way,

this the first of many little experiments
out here in the warm summer woods --
miles to go before he
sleeps, miles to
go before he sleeps.

a time like no other

"lock the door and put out the lights,
we're in for the night,"
says the sexy young hubby to his
sexy young wife. they have
been married for exactly
3 weeks. they are fucking
near constantly. they are
both very attractive
humans. he likes himself
naked. she likes herself
naked. they like each
other naked.
they like fucking.
a lot.
they do it a whole lot.
they've been married
for exactly 3 weeks,
and, while they
did it a fair amount
before they were married,
they are doing it
a WHOLE LOT
now.
**

so it is 10 pm and
all the lights
in the house
are off except
for the lights
in their bedroom and
the sexy young hubby
is cheerfully fucking
his sexy young wife,
and she is yipping with
pleasure, and he is
yelping with pleasure,
and when he spurts
his cum deep into

her, she is herself
cumming and cumming
and cumming, watching
his little nipples
with their tiny little
drops of sweat, clinging
-- oh yes the sexy
young hubby and his
sexy young wife like
doing it with the
bedroom lights on,
and no
covers over
their sweet
sexy young flesh.
**

in the morning,
over breakfast,
they look at
each other and have
a little giggle
fest -- it's all so
sickening sweet
you just want
to hug them both,
because by now
you're so in love
with them and
what they've got that
your feelings for them
could be described as
"not even healthy" --
the term "stalker" might
even be invoked,
amongst the cheerful
little chorus of the
grins and the
giggles.

flamingo waltz

the sexy red-haired college boy
undresses in front of
his bedroom window, with the blinds open.
then he masturbates. his dick is
huge, and it is so shiny it
approaches translucence.
his pubic hair is as red as the
hair on top of his handsome head. when he
spurts cum, he spurts
it onto a big old beach towel that he has
spread across the foot of his skinny little bed.
**
then he closes the blinds.
**
the show usually started at about
10:15 pm.
i was transfixed. that red pubic
hair is forever in my memory.
that big hard smooth translucent dick.
i stood outside his
apartment window, hidden
behind some shrubbery. he was in
his own apartment.
my apartment was nearby.
**
he moved out of his apartment.
one day, he was suddenly gone.
never saw him again.
several
months later, i moved out, too.
**
now,
i'm 63 years old.
i used to watch this show
when i was 27 years old. i used to watch
it nearly every night.
then i would
hurry back to my own

apartment and
masturbate as if
my life depended on it.
**

i preferred totally
naked on my back,
in bed, a rattling fan
blowing cool air across my
belly.
**

as one gets older,
one notices barns with
faded paint,
roads slick and shiny
after a pounding rain,
the branches of trees heavier with
the weight of the water
after the storm, when their
leaves are all
drenched and dripping,
the crevices in their
craggy bark infused
with little rivulets.
**

cashews, however, remain my favorite
snack food.
you just can't
go wrong with cashews -- the taste
and texture
get right in your blood.

life lessons

told to list his "likes"
the sexy big-dicked teenage boy
writes down
--football
--hamburgers
--masturbating
then scratches off
the last one
then shrugs and
puts it back.
a decision he'll soon learn to both
regret, and
appreciate.
honesty being what it is these
days, everywhere, and yet
nowhere at all.

muddy toes

i remember long ago, when i was a
skinny messy fucked-up manic depressive
teenage boy,
i used to walk naked
in the wooded hills near our house, way out
in the country.
soon i'd be
jerking off in the springtime sun
kind of proud of my nice smooth
teenage-boy body
and me feeling all sexy and
sexual and messed-up goofy weird,
not fully aware yet of
exactly what's wrong with
me the manic depression
diagnosis not
official yet, and
me just feeling weird-goofy-sexy
and the smell of my own cum
there in the springtime
sun, me
17, 16,
somewhere
in there.
now, i'm 62, and
i know i was
a mess back then, suicide
attempts hadn't happened
yet, but soon would,
dark times ahead,
and yet,
at 62, i'm
thinking
back to who i was and what
i did and things that i'll
never do again and the person

i'll never be again --
what a god-awful goofy
time, what pain, what
sweet, sweet sorrow.

reverence for falling stars

two sexy big-dicked teenage boys
are sitting side by side on the
bank of a river.
the water is flowing fast, and smells
kind of like charcoal.
"nice day," says one of
the sexy big-dicked teenage boys.
"yep, nice day," says the other
sexy big-dicked teenage boy.
**
in any contest between land and water,
it's never certain which one is older, and
will outlast the other.

i think he said his name was "lucky"

for his halloween costume,
the sexy big-dicked young man decided
to go naked. in other words, he decided he'd
"dress up" as a nudist.
this thought amused the sexy big-dicked young man
very much,
and, the first door he knocked on,
a young woman answered.
"trick or treat," said
the sexy naked big-dicked young man.
he held out a little brown paper sack,
and waited for his treat.
the young woman slammed the door in his face.
he turned and walked down the sidewalk.
very soon, a police car showed up.
two cops hurried over to the
sexy naked big-dicked young man,
and one of the cops wrapped a blanket
around him.
"you're under arrest," said the cop who
had wrapped him up with the blanket.
"indecent exposure."
"but it's halloween," said the
sexy naked big-dicked young man,
"and this is my costume. i'm 'dressed
up' as a nudist. get it?"
and then the young man
laughed, quite charmingly.
"yeah yeah," said the other cop. "very funny.
but you're STILL under arrest for indecent exposure."
and so the two cops and the sexy big-dicked young man
who was wrapped up in the blanket
drove to the police station/jail.
they booked the sexy big-dicked young man
and issued him some jail clothes and
put him a cell and told him to
get dressed.
the sexy big-dicked young man

refused. in fact, he threw off the blanket,
and stood there sexy, naked, big-dicked,
with a full horny erection that suddenly looked,
in fact, like it was made entirely out of
bone, and then encrusted with
brittle knobby chunks of tortoise shell.
there then ensued what seemed to be
a general melting and fusing of flesh,
and the creature that
the sexy naked big-dicked young man
had become kicked out the bars
of the cell's window, unfurled
a pair of wings, and flew off into the
starry night-time sky.
"happy halloween," were the parting words
the two cops heard, as the goosebumps
seized them, and covered their
pale municipal flesh.

who is god

a long silence

a sexy naked big-dicked teenage boy

ordering from catalogs

autumn

you're in love
you're dancing naked

red leaves blow down from the trees

and

touch your skin

idealist

the smiling face of opportunity greeted him
in the mirror as he stared at the stubble that
he would shave off later in the morning,
if he was in the mood, that is.
oh it was certainly nice
being
a sexy naked big-dicked young man
staring at his own face in the mirror
in the morning, trying to decide
if he was even going to shave at all,
knowing the day
was ripe with promise,
dripping juicy like a golden peach with
yellowjackets flying all around it
just waiting to take a sharp chitinous-jawed
bite.
for now, though,
the sexy naked big-dicked young man
just looked at the stubble on the
jaws of his handsome face,
peeked at the rest of his good-looking body
examined the nice heft of his dick and balls
licked his sensuous lips
and
pictured himself
watching himself
shave that stubble off his face,
the
morning glowing like a goddamn peach,
ripe for the picking,
if there were someone there, that is,
to pick that goddamn thing.
**
soon it became late afternoon.
the sexy naked big-dicked young man
was drunk again,
lying on the floor on his back,
tugging on his big smooth dick, readying

himself for yet another good gushy
sloppy cum-spurting
orgasm, pausing in his tugging,
every now and then to touch
his face, still covered with stubble
no he'd never gotten around to
shaving, never gotten around
to much at all today, except, this
this THIS the lying naked on
his broad sexy back tugging
on his big sturdy dick,
spurting wad after wad of
hot gooey cum -- a nice way to
spend the
entire day -- why shave and
interrupt the flow, so to speak --
the
moon rising now, he could see it
through his open window
the sky the color of a fresh green
pickle
like his gramma used to make
back
when
he was just a wee little kid -- he
thought about that
pickle now, as he
tugged and tugged, and
didn't cum and didn't cum -- and
in fact he wanted to cum but
it wasn't happening this time --
and so he stood up
and went to the kitchen,
thinking about his
grandma's pickles,
thinking back to when
he was just a
kid, back to
when he
first

poked the
tip of one of those nice firm
green pickles,
oh so gently,
into his tight little asshole,
pink-lipped alleyway, the
vinegar stingy, but in
a good kind of way,
his hand
on the refrigerator
door now, his thoughts
minty green.

the erasmusic of buttered lunacy

"certainly the grass grows greener amongst michelangelo's
forget-me-nots, and the houseflies on the dust of the moon hover lightly,
waiting for powdered sugar to be sprinkled upon their pink
fluffy cupcakes," says the sexy naked big-dicked
college boy english major to the sexy naked
big-dicked college boy physics major.
both sexy naked big-dicked college boys, the english
major and the physics major, are
in a meadow, on top of a mountain, lying
on a big soft quilt.
"what the HELL are you talking about NOW??" says the
physics major. the sun is bright and
shining, and the two sexy naked big-dicked
college boys are
head-over-heels in love with each other.
"oh sometimes i just like to let words roll
around any way they want to on the tip of
my tongue," says the english major.
"but you DO talk a lot of total nonsense sometimes,
you know that don't you?" says the physics major.
"and you just love that about me, now don't you?"
replies the english major.
"welllll..." says the physics major, but
now the two sexy naked big-dicked college boys,
the english major and the physics major,
are kissing and hugging and rubbing
every naked part of themselves against virtually every
naked part of each other.
they soon each spurt about a gallon of hot wet
sloppy cum,
and then they lie there, side by side,
staring up into the sky.
"the concentricity of a ring of jellybeans,
arranged on a square pottery plate, is
a joy to behold when the bath water
is soapy, and bubbly, and gently warm in the tub," says
the english major.
"really?" says the physics major.
"it's the absolute truth," says the english major. "as true

as the twists and turns of magpie fate and strawberry dreams."
"suppose i just kiss your nipples?" says the physics major.
"rudimentary tactile pleasure then is it?" says the english major.
"the garden of earthly delights and secret
firefly messages scribbled in the clouds at night,"
replies the physics major,
astonishing
them both with that
sudden gush of, for him,
glowing and atypical verbal imagery.
"well i'll be damned," says the english major.
"want some mustard
on that hot
dog big boy?" says the physics major.
for
oh my yes, it is indeed a mighty fine day in paradise:
the clouds are big and fluffy,
hovering there now in
the silence, as
nipples are licked,
and kissed, and
licked again.

ullage*

all the pretty flowers dipped their heads
in the rain, as if worshipping, or
afraid, or cold.
it was difficult for him to tell which
was their main emotion,
as he stood amongst them, wet,
cold, and shivering,
wearing only a t-shirt and
blue jeans, and nothing else. he was
barefooted.
he had just recently turned 26 years old.
he was 6 feet 4 inches
tall, skinny, handsome,
soaking wet and cold. oh, yes,
how well he knew:
spring rains can be very
cold. and this was one of them.
so he stood there shivering,
looking down at the wet bent dripping
flowers. he addressed one of
the daffodils: "i'm thinking
of quitting my job, moving
to a tropical island,
running around naked all
the time, fucking every
boy who wants me."
the daffodil replied: "but,
alas, when
the rain stops, you'll
still be standing here,
won't you? waiting
for me to tell you
what to do."
the 6-foot-4-inch-
tall-skinny-handsome young man
said: "that would be just
like me, wouldn't it?"
"yes, indeed, it certainly

would," said the wet, smug
daffodil.
the rain continued.
all the flowers
dripped, bent,
looking toward the
earth, as if there
lay the final answer.
"or perhaps i should
just go back inside
and have a drink?"
said the 6-foot-4-inch-
tall-skinny-handsome young man.
"yes, do," said the
daffodil. "and then you
should play with yourself:
but don't stick anything
up your butt this time.
that's just gross."
"i promise," said
the 6-foot-4-inch-
tall-skinny-handsome young man,
a twinkle in his eye--for he had
lied before, and
not to just
some goddamned flower.
he left the garden,
and
his footprints quickly filled
up with water,
even his toeprints,
even the prints left
by his little toes, yes,
even those,
as well.

*the amount of liquid within a container that
is lost during shipment or storage.

blessed be

as the sun rose over the valley,
the jolly green giant woke up
from a sexy dream, and spurted
about 3 gallons of thick
gooey light-green cum.
then he wiped himself off
with about 50 heads of
frilly leafy lettuce.
**
meanwhile, in the distant
city,
two sexy young men
could stand the suspense
of their chaste relationship no more,
and suddenly sucked each
other off, and quite
vigorously, too. in fact,
their
enthusiasm was
energy squared by light frequency sent digital.
**
later that day,
these same two sexy young
men ate green-giant-brand
green peas for dinner,
and everybody felt
good about that.
the golly green giant
himself sensed what
was going on, and smiled as
the sun was setting. he
pulled off his
little green tunic.
it slept silently
beside him all through
the night, just like
a little green dragon,
with pretty green scales. in

the morning, though, it wrapped itself around
his balls, and squeezed gentle pulses,
until the green giant shot another
great bit wad.
**

at the same time the
green giant was spurting,
the two sexy young men
sat up in bed,
blinked, and then
pounced on each other
with the certainty of
troglodytes, going in for
the deep zone,
nothing to stop them
but the fabric
of urgency, twisted, and then
laid on its side, like
rows of corn, after a
thunderstorm, some of the stalks
still standing, though,
but wet, and almost slimy.
**

when the green giant stood
up and put on his
tunic, the
sun experienced an
eruptive episode,
smoke alarms went
off everywhere, and
eighteen kettles of
fish bubbled
insolently,
as if to
emphasize the
nature of
stratospheric uncertainty,
love sequestered, and
huge green nipples,
nevertheless tanned slightly pink,

though, by the outdoorsy nature
of this sweet
little nugget of a
job.

the sweet smell of decay

some of us got together and decided to buy
an old mental hospital that we found in the woods.
it was in pretty bad shape.
some walls had collapsed.
there was water damage.
the forest had worked its way right into
the central lawn and up against the
main complex of buildings.
we contributed what we could.
a penny here, a nickel there.
it wasn't much of a down payment, but the
current owners didn't seem very set on the particulars.
we told them we'd get the rest of the money from the bank.
we told the bank we were going to turn
the place into a luxury hotel out there in the middle
of the wilderness with a five-star restaurant
and top-quality service.
the bank was most agreeable and gave
us the necessary funds.
i'm afraid some of us didn't work very hard to whip
the place into shape.
some of us spent most of the days just wandering
in the woods, looking at the signs of decay.
there was an old wall way out way away from
the main complex that didn't seem to be there for anything.
it was crumbly and big, and old vines and trees wriggled
all over it.
some of us spent a lot of time in our rooms, trying to
get things organized and livable. ironically,
some of the rooms were already in really good
shape when we took over the place.
nice furniture, no mildew, good-looking carpets,
bathrooms immaculate and no rust stains,
those rooms went fast, there was kinda a stampede
on those rooms,
my old college roommate and i got one of those
rooms, he mostly wanted it for himself, but
decided he wasn't going to get rid of me

very easily, so he'd just accept the situation,
some of us tried to learn to cook, but
we weren't very good at it. some of
us spent a lot of time sweeping the hallways,
some of us really were good with hammers and
saws and sanders and power-tools and they
made a lot of progress. my old college
roommate was among that group,
i was kinda with the floor sweepers, kinda
with the guys who went out by themselves
and wandered in the woods on nice
days, sometimes one of us would run
into the other one and we'd take off
all our clothes and lie down beside
each other and we'd jerk off together,
talking admiringly, yet, with just a tinge
of bitterness, about the guys who were doing
the sawing and sanding and power-tool
using. then we'd get dressed and wander off
on our separate ways, and eventually
we'd end up back at the old mental
hospital. my old college roommate
was having less and less use for
me, he worked hard all day and
his muscles were getting bigger
and he was sore and cranky.
he was making noises that i should
do more work or move out. i kept out
of his way as much as possible,
and, in fact, i really did start doing
my work better, those hallways were
constantly clean and looked real darn good,
but i was still a little leery of him, and
for quite a few weeks i had developed
the habit of coming in late when he was already
asleep in his bed and watching
him sleep, occasionally he slept
on his back with just a sheet
over him and his big erect dick
lifted the sheet well above his

belly and it just kinda bounced
lightly with the pulse of his erection.
eventually the renovation was done.
we hired a really good chef and
a whole crew to run the restaurant.
guests began to come down the
old winding road through the woods and to
eat in the restaurant and to spend
the night in rooms in our old renovated
mental hospital. sometimes guests would
go out walking in the woods. sometimes
a solitary guest would go out alone,
and one afternoon a few of us
happened upon a guest all alone in the woods
and we asked him if he wanted to
take off all of his clothes and jerk off
with us and he said yes. he was
only 17 or 18 yrs old and he was
very very beautiful, with a really
big monstrous cock, and we all
paid quite a lot of attention to
him as he stripped and jerked off.
it was enjoyable, there in the
deep dark woods watching him
and each other jerking off,
although he was by far the
most fun to watch. he had
a great face and lots of muscles
and his fully erect cock was very thick and
probably at least 11 inches long,
maybe longer.
i think everybody came two or three
times that day. then we all got
dressed and went our different
ways and all arrived back at
the old mental hospital by separate
routes. the next day, the cute boy who had jerked
off with us left along with his parents.
the weeks went by. those who
sawed and sanded and

used power-tools called meetings
and told us we were making
a nice profit, that things were
going well, our duties became
more systematic, it was acknowledged, for instance,
in fact, my old college roommate said it quite
eloquently, that i was an excellent sweeper
of the halls, that i kept them really clean,
and that i should be assigned that duty
permanently. i flushed bright red
as he talked, and that night, when he
was asleep on his back, and i was watching
his big erect cock lift his nice white
sheet above his nice flat belly,
i pulled down the sheet very very carefully
and just as it cleared his thighs, he
opened his eyes, and he told me that if
i wanted it that bad, go ahead,
give him a nice slow handjob, and
that's what i did, he came all over his
belly and i wiped it off of him with a
nice warm soapy wash rag from our
bathroom, and then i rinsed his belly
with fresh water, and then i dried
his belly, and pulled the sheet
back over him and he went to sleep
in his bed and i went to sleep in my
bed, after first jerking myself off
as silently as possible, i don't think
my old college roommate heard
a thing. weeks went by.
profits were up. we all had
food and a roof over our heads
and sometimes nobody did
hardly any work and in spite
of the fact that those who sawed
and sanded and used power-tools
held meetings and yelled at various
ones of us, it was noted that
sometimes the power-tool guys

didn't do all that much work themselves
on certain days, there was
general dissatisfaction from
the kitchen, the head chef quit,
and went to another job, and took
most of his staff with him,
there was a general feeling
of tension about the place,
the old mental hospital was
not attracting the customers
it once did, sometimes there
were days when there were
no guests at all, and some
of us fixed sandwiches for ourselves
and for everybody else, and sometimes
everybody had to fix their own
sandwiches, my old college
roommate started spending
a lot of time just laying about
the room and sometimes
he lay on his bed stark naked
and expected me to give
him handjobs without even
being asked to, i wasn't
liking him as much as i used
to, and sometimes i didn't
even come back to the room
at night, but lay near the old
wall way out in the woods,
listening to things move amongst
the fallen leaves in the darkness,
sometimes i took off all my
clothes and lay there spread
eagle on the leaves staring
up into the sky, there were
tears in my eyes, and as
the night wore on, i would
make growling sounds in
my throat to answer the
growling sounds i occasionally

heard around me, and then
i'd get dressed and go back
to the room and shower,
eventually my old college roommate
left the old mental hospital altogether,
and i had the room to myself,
for a period of time
there were no more guests at all
at the old mental hospital,
except one night the 17-or-18
yr-old guy who had jerked off
with us in the woods came back
and some of us ended up jerking
off with him in the old shock-therapy
room while we smeared jergens
body lotion all over him,
he left that same night,
his eyes were wild and
the tip of his tongue was
between his lips, eventually
there were only a few of us left in
the old mental hospital in the woods,
we ate coldcuts and bread,
one of the power-tool guys
was evidently pretty rich and a little off his
rocker, and he kept on
funding the place, but there
were no extravagances, it
was pretty basic, out there
in the woods. sometimes,
growling in the night alone
in my room, i heard others
growling, too, sometimes
i'd creep outside the door
of somebody i heard growling,
and then i'd try the doorknob,
generally it wouldn't open,
but sometimes it would,
and i'd go on in, and we'd
just sit down together, and

we'd talk about what
was going to happen next,
and we wouldn't have a clue,
we'd say we missed the good
ole days when there were
lots of guests and the restaurant
was still operating, and i'd confess
that i felt like everything was
going to hell, we were all
in one big long tailspin that
we were never going to get out
of, often the guy whose room i
happened to be in at the moment
would agree, and then sometimes
we'd just lay there not saying
a word, too tired to lift a finger,
too tired for much of anything,
eventually the power-tool guy
with the money moved out,
winter was coming, food
was running low, but
we stayed on anyway,
and every now and then,
guests still came, not
of the quality we were used to,
and not in the numbers we'd
once grown to expect,
but we were constantly surprised
by what people were looking for
out there in the middle of
the woods, our old mental
hospital looming grey and sinister
there in the clearing,
exactly what they are looking for
has never been readily apparent
to any of us, certainly not to me
anyway, and they tolerate questionable conditions
far better than i'd have
ever expected.

the dignity of cloth napkins

the sexy naked big-dicked boys are
out roaming the forests. their eyes are
praeternaturally bright and their teeth
are so white that they're dazzling.
the sexy naked big-dicked boys attack
wild animals and tear them into pieces and
swallow them raw. they are having the
time of their lives, these sexy naked
big-dicked boys, roaming around
wild and wild-eyed, taking what they want.
nothing can stop them.
after a successful day in which they
fell 3 deer and 2 wild pigs, as well as an elk, a moose,
and a mountain lion,
the sexy naked big-dicked boys
are lounging around beside a stream,
all of them masturbating
while they eat,
their big dicks hard
and throbbing and
periodically spurting out
big gooey plumes of hot runny cum.
then, after dining
and spurting cum,
a relatively peaceful mood hovers about the place,
and they settle down for conversation.
the sexy naked big-dicked boy who's
kinda in charge tonight -- they took a vote -- he also happens
to be the cutest guy there -- maybe effected the outcome
of the vote, maybe not -- anyhow, this guy gets to
select the topic for this evening's
discussion. when he announces it is "the history
of bipolar disorder and its treatment," at first
everyone has a real good chuckle, until they
realize he's goddamn serious.
then, out come the textbooks,
and it's right down to business.

missed opportunities

watercolor the pizzas while the
feral tomcat wades across the stream.
the sky is about to open up and
drop about a ba-zillion raindrops,
but that hasn't happened yet.
the little silver-colored fish
are swimming in schools of
about a hundred fish each.
the tomcat has learned that
attack is useless, for the
little fishies are quite
impossible. might as well
try to eat air.
**

once, when the sexy naked big-dicked
teenage boy was
out walking,
he and the big
ole yellow feral tomcat had eyeballed each
other,
and decided, evidently, that
they were too much alike
to cause any real difficulty.
**

it was, ultimately, the sexy naked big-dicked
teenage boy
who captured the little silver fishies
in his minnow trap.
and, even though the tomcat begged
and yowled,
the boy wouldn't give him any.
**

after that,
they remained life-long enemies.
the boy went on to become a great fisherman -- he
fished rain or shine.

often the
tomcat
sat in the rain,
his ears dripping the bitter
gray water of those who have been shamed,
but not conquered.

creosote pineapple

let us go
into the realm
of elevated emotional states, and quickened heartbeat,
and big thick erections that occur so often,
they are practically every quarter hour.
**
its quick jounces and its apparent pulsating urgency.
**
let us go into his bedroom, where,
sometimes, after a
nap, and all alone,
in front of his own bedroom mirror,
the sexy naked big-dicked teenage boy
alters the flow of blood
to his heart,
and re-arranges his position so that
his dick points off more toward
one side, than toward the middle.
**
just a swivel of the
hips, really,
one buttock a little more
relaxed, than
tense.

both of us 20 years old, him & me

there is nothing more to be said.
**
there is always something more to be said.
**
i need to talk with him.
**
but mainly i want to lick the tip of
his dick and feel his warm cum
spurting into my mouth, feel his warm cum
slosh around on my slobbery tongue.
**
i am 20 years old. so is
he.
**
he is straight. i am trying
to be straight, too, but almost
certainly i am gay.
he is a swimmer on the college
swim team. he is gorgeous,
sweet, gentle, friendly.
i am almost certainly in love
with him.
i am pretty good-looking, too.
long, lean, lithe, athletic.
we play a lot of tennis
together, him and me.
we look good together, too.
**
i need to talk with him. even though
we talk hours and hours
and hours, but it is not enough.
it is never enough.
we talk while we shower together
in the university gym.
we talk while we backpack together
on hikes on the weekends.
we talk while we're getting dressed.
we talk while we're walking to class.

**

no matter how much we talk,
it is not enough.
**

we are twenty years old.
he is gorgeous, his face handsome,
his cheeks ruddy, his dick big
and sturdy.
i am pretty good-looking myself.
**

there is nothing more to be said.
**

there is always something more to be said.
**

i need to talk to him. i want
to lick the tip of his dick.
i want to watch him spurt cum.
i want him to watch me spurt cum.
**

i don't like his girlfriends, even
though they are nice enough.
i am jealous of them. i am
jealous of the time they
take from me.
**

i am 20 years old.
so is he. we are roommates.
we are in college. we are
young and our energy never
ends. we run laps and play
tennis and since it is
not swimteam season
he doesn't have to swim
so he is able to spend
that time with me.
**

i watch him sleep.
i jerk off while he sleeps.
i want him to wake up and
catch me doing that, but

he is a sound sleeper.
at least he pretends to
be. if he's ever caught
me jerking off, he's
not let on.
**
we need to talk. i need
to talk. we talk a lot.
but it is never ever enough.
**
once i blurted out to him that
i loved him. he seemed
kinda taken aback, then,
he was a good sport
about it, and said
he loved me, too. kind of in
his "aw shucks" voice.
**
things go on like that.
**
i am 20. so is he.
we look good together.
we need to talk.
i need to talk.
**
i need.
**
there's nothing more to
be said.
**
there's always something
more to be said.
**
i need to touch his dick.
i need to feel him spurt his
cum into my mouth.
i need for us to sit on
the couch naked and
watch each other jerk off.
i need for us to jerk each

other off. i'm sure his
touch on my
dick would be warm, but gentle.
i'm sure my touch on his
dick would be crazy fast and
entirely too eager.
**

we are 20 years old.
it is early in the morning.
we are playing tennis.
the sound of the
court: thwack. thwack.
**

we need to talk.
**

i love him.
i am in pain.
he is beautiful.
i look pretty good myself.
we look good together.
**

i need to talk.
**

why do i seem to feel
every emotion through my
dick? why does the sound
of
his nice deep voice
resonate in my dick?
**

i feel everything in my
dick.
**

joy, sorrow, love,
hate--i feel them
all in my dick.
**

i spurt cum and think
of him.
**

i hate his girlfriends.
**
can't we talk, just him
and me?
**
i need to talk.
**
there's nothing more to
be said.
**
there's always something
more to be said.
**
how often does he spurt cum? i
wish he would
tell me tell me tell me tell me.
**
i need to talk.
i know we talk a lot, but
please, let's just
talk some more.
**
no matter how
much we say
to each other,
it is never enough
talking all night
only whets my
insatiable appetite
for him and
him and
the more he's there
the more i'll want
this will never end
this will always hurt
this will always
be a big slurry
of lust, and joy,
and pain.
we'll be 20 years old

forever, him and me, the
sunrises and
sunsets flashes
of light and dark,
twists of tenderness and
urgency,
the light shining behind his
ears makes
them glow pink,
then nearly red,
i look into his crystal
blue eyes
as the sunlight
immolates first one, then
the other,
of his sacred, sexy,
delicately pink ears.

taxonomy

speculation runs rampant.
is THIS movie star gay? is THAT movie star gay?
the truth is, ALL artists are suspect.
actors, poets, short-story writers, novelists.
painters. sculptors. potters. chefs.
builders of installations.
i'm not sure whether MORE artists tend
to be gay than members of the regular population,
but, my guess is that it's likely to be so.
and who's an artist anyway? anyone
who calls himself or herself an
artist is an artist. now, as to
whether he or she is a GOOD artist,
or a BAD artist, or an
artist who's somewhere in between, well,
LOTS of people get to apply those adjectives,
and they seem to ABSOLUTELY RELISH doing so.
(in fact, you, dear reader, probably kinda
relish it yourself, now don'tcha?)
but, yeah, speculation really
does run rampant about movie stars,
doesn't it? is HE gay? is SHE a lesbian?
isn't he Bi? people just seem
endlessly fascinated by stuff like
that, don't they?
for me, it's the most fun
to speculate about the really outrageously
good-looking male movie stars.
the ones who look so great my
eyes nearly pop out and my ears kinda
want to bleed when he appears half-naked
on screen. oh it's certainly fun
to imagine him all the way naked, and
coupling with
a naked male friend possessing equal or
perhaps (if possible) even more
lovely and sexy physical attributes.
of course, if he's a REALLY GOOD

actor, if the movies he's in
are ABSOLUTELY BRILLIANT, then,
well, i'm putty, lost, adrift,
awhirl in daydream ville:
gay, hot-looking, talented,
brilliant, making good art.
situations like that, if my mind
were a pony express rider,
i'd already be there,
the mail would already be
delivered, and everybody
who was expecting to hear
from somebody would've heard.
they'd be standing around
in their chaps, kinda teary
eyed and happy, jaws bristly,
fingernails rough and dirty.

alarmist

suddenly it is night, and yet we continue
to deny that the swift sure certainty
of our own demise is at hand.
galaxies glitter in the darkness,
crickets chirp and twitter under
the dank mist beneath the
rotting mulch of the best gardens
in the best parts of town.
99.9 percent of all species that
ever lived are now extinct. and
yet we continue to think this
means nothing to us. we need
to think this means nothing
to us. we want to think
this means nothing to us.
**

up in his room, alone in the
dark, the sexiest most scrumptious
long-legged broad-shouldered smooth-backed
tiny-nippled big-dicked teenage boy
you could ever imagine quietly
beats off underneath the covers.
the spermy mess of his own cum
soon covers his fingers, and,
all at once, the whole process is
so beautiful to him that
he breaks into tears, lying
naked and spermy and clammy-hot under the
covers in his dark room,
the crickets chirping outside
his window, galaxies spinning
and whirling millions of
miles away.
**

yes, suddenly it
is night, and we are truly frightened.
the only thing that makes sense
is temporary and fleeting pleasure.

yet, can 30 years of pleasure
be construed as equaling nothing
of importance? can 30 years of
pleasure be considered to
be a bad thing? all leads
to nothing, anyway. the
demise will happen. nothing
we can do or think about
will stop it.
why not try not to think
about it? why not
give yourself over to absolute
pleasure, swim the deep waters
of the sins of the flesh?
another drink, perhaps.
or two, or three.
or 8.
**

but, alas, now,
your mission, should you
decide to accept it,
is over. oh yes, quite suddenly it
is night, the crickets
have stopped chirping, and
the mulch around those fancy
hybridized roses is
now festering with mildew,
only just beginning to make
friends with
the roots.

prettier

the world sits like a water-lily pad draped over the
back of a turtle.
sexy bare-chested movie stars wander freely about,
talking with their hands.
cattle munch delicately only the tenderest most
succulent blades of grass.
**
the turtle yawns and stretches.
this water-lily pad of a world wobbles and weaves.
**
sweetly pink and naked boys and girls
frolic together in the waves.
camels drink their fill, discover the shadiest spots in the oasis.
rain falls. the turtle blinks, lumbers
toward the apple pie sitting on
the window sill.
**
heads bob up and down; hiccups occur everywhere.
**
then, calmness returns. we all go along
for the ride.

peace peace peace

when the tv's on and the bourbon's just easing
its way into my system, creeping through my
blood vessels toward my fingertips and my earlobes,
ah, this is when the rest of the day
recedes into the background, details
dislodging themselves from my brain,
so-called pressing problems displaced by
a feeling of well-being and comfort.
**
when the cute young man on the tv screen
takes off his shirt and strides
with masculine stride from point a to point b,
wearing only those tight-fitting faded ole blue
jeans of his, and the bourbon is really
absorbing nicely directly from my tongue tip
to my brain stem (biologically possible
or not! it sure feels that way sometimes),
then, ah yes then, it's nice to be
alive, gently buzzed, watching a
sexy half-naked young man walk
non-threateningly across the tv screen,
and the ice in my glass makes such
a charming tinkle, it's almost like
a song, a good one, with a sweet
melody, and a kind gentle heart.
**
jim beam bourbon n canada dry ginger ale,
gently mixed, over ice: pretty & lightly amber
in the glass, what else do you want me to say?
well, i do understand why people drink,
and i understand why i drink, and i understand
why i'll probably never quite quit, even
though sometimes, it seems like
some kind of idea, you know, just
for a change.

attitude

the enjoyment of orgasm is a funny thing.
**

for some people, the only thing that comes (no
pun intended teehee) close to the pleasure of
orgasm is the pleasure of being drunk,
or of being under the influence of some
illegal substance. for other people,
the only thing that comes (there we go again)
close to the pleasure of orgasm is the pleasure
of having an orgasm WHILE being drunk or
WHILE being under the influence of
some illegal or barely
legal substance.
**

people are funny. for example: take a
tall good-looking big-dicked sexy young man.
he stands there naked jerking off
all alone in front the big full-length
mirror on the back of his bedroom door.
he's having an incredibly good time,
standing there jerking off, and
he hasn't even had his orgasm yet.
he knows that having the orgasm is
gonna be the best part,
though, and when it starts happening,
it doesn't bother
him a bit that his
pleasure is being enhanced
by the act of watching himself have
an orgasm in front of
his mirror. should he be bothered
that he likes watching himself come?
is there something, well, gay, about
enjoying watching himself come?
**

people are funny when it comes
to their reaction to their pleasure
at having an orgasm. some people

just can't get over it, never want
to do another thing besides having
an orgasm for the rest of their
whole entire lives. and yet,
they're just not put together
that way, physiologically i mean;
they can't just have an orgasm
all day long every day every
waking moment. and yet, that's
what these people want. pleasure
all the time. hedonists, that's
what they are.
**

other folks, once or twice a
month seems to be enough
orgasming for them. and even then they
worry that that's just too disruptive
to their normal routine of having
an even-keel kind of life; or maybe,
too, they're afraid that having an
orgasm is sinful, because it's
just so much pleasure at one
time, and centered in one forbidden
place--but that's a whole 'nother
can of worms, isn't it?
**

anyhow, right now, right this very minute
somewhere on earth, there are
no doubt two tall good-looking
big-dicked sexy young men
capably and enthusiastically
rubbing each other's cocks and
waiting eagerly to spurt their cum.
**

they won't have to wait long, even
with the sound of somebody protesting
outside their door -- hey,
if you think people are funny about
how they react to their own orgasms,
well, that's nothing

compared to the way they react to
other people's orgasms, now is it?

regrets only

space aliens kidnapped my brain,
stuffed it down their pants,
came on it with their long slimy pencil-thin
dicks.
yes, space aliens kidnapped my brain,
then showed it a good time up
there amongst the planets and alongside
the stars. space aliens got-off repeatedly
on my kidnapped brain, then politely returned
it cum-drippy, and moon-struck,
comet-tail-dusted, and stellar-delighted.
**
now, with my kidnapped-by-space-aliens-
and-fucked-by-space-aliens's-pencil-thin-dicks brain
put back smoothly inside my head,
i seem restless, worried,
distracted -- lost, violated, and
raw -- adrift in the universe, severed
like chicken heads
pecking each other to death.
**
the moon is a werewolf, and
i am the silver bullet.
my toenails have turned gray,
and pedicure seems useless.

that word

the fire and ice of love and desire
may be simplified by the term "addiction" but
that seems unfair and dry and clinical.
love and desire may not, or
should not, be simplified
so easily and glibly. the sexy naked young
man lying on his back in the middle
of a sunny meadow tugging on his
big smooth cock while the rays
of the sun caress and love
and heat him up is not merely
"addicted" to solitary sex in
the sunshine. he is enveloped
by everything about the moment,
the sensation of his dick
responding to his fingers on it,
the sensation of the sunshine
on his nipples and navel
and balls and knees and toes.
he is enveloped, caught up in
it all, in everything about
everything about it.
to reduce all this
to an "addiction" of some
sort is disingenuous, to
say the least. to what
is this sexy naked young
man "addicted"? being naked?
masturbating? the feel of
the sunshine on his naked
skin? the feel of the
meadowgrass on his butt?
or is it, perhaps,
that his so-called "addiction"
is to complete and utter
oneness with everything,
sex, nature, sun, meadow,
heat on skin, sunlight in eyes,

texture of dick skin, texture
of finger skin against dick
skin, exquisiteness of
having balls pulled up
tight and greedy
against body instead
of dangling half-interested
and lazy? no. this all
goes well beyond the
application of the
term "addiction" -- even
though he does this, all
of it, alone, over
and over and over, dozens
of time a month during
the sizzling summer, when
his heart is hungry
for the taste of
the universe.

got time for a quickie

when the wine is on the lips
and miracle-gro is in the flower pot,
there's a moment of purity, clarity:
fevered, frantic thoughts are banished.
it's just you, the wine, and the
ivy.
**

tranquility is so quiet and peaceful
it almost seems a constant state of being,
instead of just a short reprieve.
**

you wonder why it can't always be
like this: the wine feels warm and good
in your belly; you wonder if
the miracle-gro feels warm and good
in the little vessels that
nourish the ivy, that make it grow,
that make it thrive, and, that quite simply,
let it exist.
**

you've had it with complexity.
you've had it with complications. but now,
it's just the wine, and the miracle-gro, and
the ivy.
**

you breathe in. you breathe out.
the hair on the back of your
arms is but a quiet and ornery
distraction, blond, wispy,
delicate as a piece of toast.

horsepower and the art of mustang maintenance

when well maintained,
cars still go quite fast even when
they're just drifting, such as when the driver's
foot is off the accelerator.
**
sometimes his car drifts; sometimes
it accelerates; but, at all times, it
is still going very very fast.
**
in fact, the cute guy driver
who is getting a blow job
says: "even when we're drifting,
we're still going really really fast."
**
and the cute guy passenger who
is giving the cute guy driver
the blow job lifts his lips
away from the cute guy driver's
great big saliva-slicked-up cock
for just a moment
and says: "yes, that's true: even
when we're drifting, we're still going
really really fast."
**
when the cute guy driver cums
and starts spurting a seemingly
endless series of cum globules
into the cute guy passenger's mouth,
and the cute guy passenger swallows and
swallows and swallows,
the car goes very very fast, then
drifts, but never moves slowly.
in fact, the momentum is always
more than adequately
maintained.
**
of course,
the best sexual adventures are often

devoid of any technological advancements
whatsoever (for example: raw naked sex in
the wilderness never
goes out of style),
but,
no matter what the demagogues tell you,
no matter what they preach,
and no matter what the manuals advise,
a blow job at 75 mph
always means those horses
are gonna
neigh.

oligocene chastity

while wiling away the hours,
the sexy naked big-dicked teenage boy
likes to tug on his big hard sturdy dick,
and spurt big sloppy gobs of hot gooey cum.
**
also, he runs many miles alone in
the bright sunny forest.
he gets stronger and sexier
and even better looking.
**
also, he likes shrimp puffs.
**
now you take yer average
shrimp puff
and savor it with
the tip of your tongue.
yer teeth crunching
on it till
there's next to nothing
there -- a bit of
wet dust in your
mouth -- and
that's all.
**
doesn't seem like
the average
sexy naked big-dicked teenage boy
would be "into"
shrimp puffs.
**
but he is.
**
life's kinda like that.
**
unexpected, barely
semi-logical.
**
you wish everything made

more sense than it actually
does.
**
but there he sits.
eating shrimp puffs.
**
and it's not even noon.

the scarcity of ripe peaches

the sexy naked big-dicked teenage boy
notices the shape
of the lamp shade
on the lamp
on his desk,
cylindrical,
but not perfectly so. in fact,
the lamp shade is kind of deformed.
he doesn't like that. in fact,
he gets pissed off,
senses depression about to
settle in, quietly,
primly, like
it's been
invited to fill in a
hole in the back
of his head.
who'd come to his funeral,
he wonders, as
he makes the wise decision
to chop off all his
pubic hair,
lands in curly tufts
on his feet, now his
discarded pubes look like
little furry critters,
ticklish on the tops of his
monster-thin
toes.

wahoo!

when i was a teenager,
i used to disappear into the woods near our house,
take off all my clothes, and jerk off,
repeatedly, sometimes 3 or 4 times
in a single afternoon. i remember
i'm spurting what felt like
two gallons of cum, all hot and gooey
and runny, and i'm all hot and sweaty and
good-looking, and my dick is hard nearly
all the time, and i'm kind of in a state
of orgiastic madness.
**
back then, i was also a
manic depressive suicidal mess.
soon to be institutionalized.
**
but, for those few hours there young and
naked and jerking off in the woods,
everything was nice,
the world was good,
and life didn't seem
nearly so crazy.

do you say "supper" or "dinner"?

magritte the wallpaper and turn out the lights.
confess your sins to anyone who will listen.
promise to be good every single minute of every single day.
if you've been doing something bad, swear that you'll
stop it at once, and swear that you'll never ever do it again.
stick to your diet. watch your alcohol intake.
watch dirty movies only if they have
some meaningful artistic statement to make.
just get yourself together!
**
while walking down the road to complete and
total recovery,
the sexy naked big-dicked young man
told himself that he needed to stop
all sorts of things that he'd been doing.
too much drinking. too much
masturbating. too much
cynicism. too much criticizing
everything and everyone. he
needed to develop a sweeter nature.
a kinder attitude.
a more forgiving stance in the world.
soon the sexy naked big-dicked young man
sat down on a big smooth rock in
the middle of the woods and
thought about all these things
while he was jerking off,
thought about all these things
as he was tugging gently and rhythmically
on his big sturdy dick,
even thought about all these
things during the all-too-brief moments when
the cum was spurting out of him.
then, the sexy naked big-dicked young man
pulled the bottle of whiskey out
of his knapsack and he sat there,
on the rock, in the middle of
the forest,

drinking whiskey and smelling
the musky scent of his
own fresh cum.
really, the world at
this moment was
all too beautiful.
how could he ever
have an
unpleasant thought
about it, or
himself, ever
ever again?
in fact, at this moment,
a bright
orange butterfly
landed on his
left nipple, and
the touch of
its delicate
and brittle little legs
made the
sexy naked big-dicked young man
grin like an
idiot, a sweet and harmless one,
with a heart
of the finest and
purest gold.

just babbling away again, enjoying the heck out of cliches, life, everything

it was the biggest dick i had ever seen
the sky opened up and poured rain on everyone
it soaked us all
and sent us scrambling for shelter
lord, please make these urges go away
the lean lithe athletic boy lay naked on his back on his
bed furiously stroking his great big cock until
it shot gob after gob of hot translucent semen
all over his taut, sweet, sweaty belly and his hard,
gorgeous, tiny-nippled chest.
somehow we've got to make sense out of all this.
cry the beloved country.
he voted in favor of pornographic art.
he has an unusual fascination with the genitalia of superheroes.
picture superman naked, on top of lois lane.
he has to pull out before he cums otherwise his supercum
would blast big gaping holes through lois's back and kill her.
did you see that guy at the other gas pump, his jeans
were so tight you could see the outline of his cock perfectly
and i do mean perfectly.
so we sat down at a nice quiet table in an out-of-the-
way cafe, and we talked for hours about everything,
about nothing, and then we went back
to my place and talked for another five hours
before i finally got his pants off and we were both rolling
around naked on the floor.
that cat is so smart, he knew exactly what to do with
his litter box the moment we showed it to him.
class, i want you to focus on me, i need your full and
undivided attention up here at the front of the room.
i'm afraid yet again he's made a mountain out of a mole hill.
birds twittered in the trees, and then there was silence,
and the hoot of an owl, and then the manitou stirred, and
walked the darkened woodlands, looking for its next victim.
he cried himself to sleep, wondering if he'd ever understand
why sex had even been invented, and why it was all he could
ever seem to think about.

he ate corn flakes for breakfast, and he felt fine until about
10 a.m., when he was hungry all over again.
alone, standing on the summit of the mountain,
he looked at the vast and distant lands spread out
before him, and he smiled triumphantly.
many of us would have called it a smug and self-satisfied grin.
because that's exactly what it was.

not really theft

my college roommate was a sexy guy.
i was pretty sure
he was straight.
and i kinda sorta knew
i was gay. but
wished i wasn't.
anyhow, my college
roommate was hot.
he was on the college
swimteam. and he looked like it.
broad back, slender waist, great abs,
tight little butt.
we shared
a one-room apartment.
i liked to watch him sleep.
my bed was only about 5 feet away
from his, and, in the dim
light that managed to
make its way in
between the closed slats of our
venetian-blind-covered window,
i could see him pretty well.
often, as i watched
him, i would
jerk off. i did it very
very quietly. and,
when i came, he
was so beautiful
i almost whimpered.
almost.
the light behind the
tip of his nose, the jut
of his chin.
the sound of his breathing,
softly in, softly out.

pollen lampshades

"in the kingdom of
the banana milkshakes," says
the sexy naked big-dicked teenage boy, wandering
the
pungent mango-scented aisles
of the all-natural supermarket,
"we must accept only the finest." and,
as the sexy naked big-dicked teenage boy
wanders the aisles in
the kingdom of juice and
pain, insanity waves its
dismissive arms, and anxieties
scatter like bluebirds. "oh let us manufacture more
organic pumpkin pies," says the
sexy naked big-dicked teenage boy,
"for paradise is but a pineapple stellar aspiration to
be gently inhaled," he says,
as store management becomes aware
of the naked boy situation there in aisle 6,
their vocal cords buzzing like
buttery bumble bees, the gently
extracted nectar of the exclusively
grown elusive organic pomegranate
the only vaguely subtle road to
all that sweet jesus honey.

sheaths and quivers

the sexy naked big-dicked teenage boy
liked to rumage around in old books, and
look at photos of ancient statues of sexy naked men.
he wanted to see some of these statues in real life.
yes, he was eager. in fact, he practically gave off vibrations.
**
one day,
the sexy naked big-dicked teenage boy
was in his room, minding his own business,
when a statue crawled in through his open window.
the statue was one of those statues that
he'd longed to see, one of those greco-etruscan-type
sexy naked men. the statue had a few chips
off one elbow, and a ding in its knee, and
a small chip off its chin, but,
other than that, the statue was pretty much
perfect. the sexy naked big-dicked teenage boy
was relieved to see that its dick hadn't been
broken off over the years, a fate that had
befallen so many other otherwise-beautiful statues
of sexy naked men.
"i think love mit," said the statue to
the sexy naked big-dicked teenage boy.
**
the sexy naked big-dicked teenage boy
didn't quite know what the statue meant by that,
but, nonetheless, he and the statue
eagerly climbed into bed.
**
after about 8 hours of non-stop sex,
the sexy naked big-dicked teenage boy
and the beautiful dinged-up statue
lay there in bed, side by side, on their backs,
staring up at the ceiling.
"wow!" said the sexy naked big-dicked teenage boy.
"meat-packing festival," said the beautiful statue.
clearly, communication was going to be a problem,
but they were confident they could work things out.

**

in the morning, inside the museum
where the statue had been on display,
the staff is puzzled by its absence, and
alarmed, too.
not one of them
imagines that that
statue simply up and
left on its own,
in search of
love in the arms of a
sexy naked big-dicked teenage boy.

**

meanwhile, back in that boy's bedroom,
the boy and the statue
just keep going at it,
eternity seems likely,
yea, verily, perhaps
even certain.

motherfuck

when the cattails are thick and fuzzy and
their strap-shaped leaves are harsh green
and leathery,
two sexy sexed-up pissed-off young men
go down to the pond beside those cattails,
and those two sexy sexed-up pissed-off
young men complain and complain and complain
and talk about things they hate and
things they despise about the world,
things they despise about people,
life, everything, and
all the while they are complaining
and saying harsh hard and really angry things,
they are drinking bourbon, and drinking
bourbon, and drinking more bourbon,
and soon they're stripping off their
shirts and sitting there on the bank
shirtless and sexy-looking and sexed-up
and cussing and saying things that they
hate about people and life and
supervisory figures and political
figures and radio talk-show figures,
and then those two sexy angry
sexed-up young men are drinking
some more bourbon, and taking off
their shoes and taking off their
socks and taking off their pants
and taking off their underpants
and standing there naked angry
big-dicked jacking off standing
there beside each other watching
each other jack off and watching
themselves jack off and saying
mean angry bitter things while
they are standing there
jacking off and
when they both spurt cum they
just stand there staring at each

other watching each
other spurt cum and then
they just stand there
naked and sheepish and
big-dicked and for the first time
that afternoon they break into
big goofy smiles and hoots of
laughter, and, at that moment,
there's a lot less tension
in the air down there at the cattail pond,
a lot less tension.

picking daisies

pacing to the left, then to
the right,
the skinny little art major college boy
practically wore down the carpet
in his room, he paced so much.
the skinny little art major college boy
was totally naked, clothes bothered
him when he was in his worry mode,
and he was sure in his worry mode
now,
ah yes indeed,
he was quite the worrier.
everything worried him.
everything made him fret.
he worried and worried and worried
and fretted and fretted and
paced to the left and
then to the right
and outside it started
to rain and then thunder and
lightning and
then gusts of wind rattled
his bedroom window and still
the skinny naked little art major college boy
went right on
pacing and worrying and fretting.
the level of his anxiety
could be described as a 10 on a
scale of 1 to 10
and when
the rain and thunder and lightning
and wind finally stopped,
the skinny naked little art major college boy
suddenly quit
pacing,
sometimes jerking off really helped
calm him down for a few moments,
he'd seen it work that way before,

more than once, in fact,
and so he
lay down on his back
on top of his bed and
tugged on his surprisingly
big vigorously rock-hard dick for a while
until he spurted cum all
over his skinny naked chest and belly
and then he wiped it off himself
and lay there staring wide-eyed
at the ceiling, and then wouldn't ya know
goddammit this time jerking off
didn't calm him down all that
much now did it
and so then
it was right back to
fretting and worrying and
fretting some more so he
got right back out of bed
and paced some more
and wore down the carpet some more
and
by now it was well after midnight
but still the skinny naked little art major college boy
couldn't sleep,
still he worried and fretted
and worried some more,
it was all just so
fucking much -- he worried
about everything, this,
that, whatever crossed his
mind, he couldn't stop
thinking about it,
this, that, the
other, just EVERYthing --
now take
Edvard Munch's
THE SCREAM, for instance --
one of them

recently sold for 55 million,
now how could anyone
sleep after that?

yes Yes YES

in the microseconds before
the sexy athletic big-dicked teenage boy
is getting ready to spurt cum,
his eyes flash like fire,
or they shut tight,
or he squints as if he's in pain.
yes, in the microseconds right
before
the sexy athletic big-dicked teenage boy
spurts cum,
he may look as though he's in pain,
but he's not.
he's in the throes of so much
pleasure that
the honesty in his eyes
is of confusion--how can there
be this much pleasure in life?
how can there be this much
pleasure on earth?
how can there be this much
pleasure going on at the
tip of my dick?
and then,
the sexy athletic big-dicked teenage boy
spurts out big hot gooey dollops of
cum,
splats them up against the wall
of the shower stall in
which he is jerking off,
and he's suddenly so
sure of the
goodness of life,
so sure of
the goodness of spurting
cum,
so sure of
the goodness of being
a sexy athletic big-dicked teenage boy,

that,
he,
just for a moment,
he's sure of everything else,
too.

zephyrs

there is nothing more beautiful than an entire
field of milkweed in full pink-sphered bloom
unless
you add to the picture two good-looking
naked young men who are taking
turns fucking each other up the ass.
**
on a wonderously clear day in early july,
in a huge milkweed field in the middle
of nowhere, they jumped out of their
car and stripped off their clothes
and just went at it, out there in
the middle of that field of milkweed.
**
later, back in the car, they wondered if
anyone had seen them out there in the field,
fucking. they wondered and wondered about that,
then gunned the engine, and,
in a matter of moments, there was only
the field, the milkweed in full pink-sphered bloom,
and the whispers of the snoopy snoopy breeze.

self portrait, sorting socks

i buy
conservatively
black socks +
shades of very dark blue socks
and then
match them up
after
they come out of
the drier.
i see myself stooping over
the socks on the neatly-made bed
just like a little old lady.

something's
not right with this picture.

the correctly colored socks
snuggle inside each other
like dicks wrapped in flesh
and right now i
am dreaming
of whole corps of strapping
big boy marines
stripping each other
bare + having
wild orgiastic
sex with
each other.

clearly the truth is that
i'm practically a barbarian writhing in the streets.

but this little old lady is standing there
stooped over the bed
sorting socks
with an efficiency that suggests
that's what
she was born to do.

the sensation of really thick breadmold

the error in the belief system of post-scriptum thinking
means that ravioli on the stovetop sometimes
boils more than it should, while little birds
in the backyard are chirping like magnets,
and three sexy naked big-dicked teenage boys
hidden away in the bedroom
are sucking on each other's big thick cum-spurting dicks,
and the yellow in the teacup is camomile, the
gentlest of all the stomach calmers.
**
there be dragons in the
land of mist and rain,
where little does the meaning of
trilobite flute-playing
impart to the interactions of
daily persimmons on their
way to market.
**
actually, persimmons are rarely
eaten anymore these days -- a shame,
really. a real darn shame.
**
after a hard frost,
persimmons are soft and mushy,
their flavor sort of pumpkinny,
as october grabs the
scarecrow, and shakes it
half to death.

trans-atlantic determination

the two sexy naked big-dicked teenage boys
have been doing sexual things with each other
all afternoon, and they have no plans
to stop.
the boys' names are
mack and bob.
**
"i love spurting cum onto your broad sleek
naked back," says mack.
"i love how it leaves a trail like
icing from a heavily-glazed cake."
bob stands there
tugging on his own big hard sturdy
dick while mack
spurts cum. mack's
cum splats onto bob's back,
and it dribbles down bob's
beautiful smooth naked back.
soon, bob begins
spurting cum himself.
it splats onto the ground
in front of him.
**
the two sexy naked big-dicked teenage boys,
mack and bob,
are standing in the midst
of a bright sunny forest. they
are miles from anywhere, and, as
far as they know, miles from anyone.
still,
though,
letting down one's guard is
never a good idea.
as the little techno-sophisticate drones
flit saucily about, snapping photographs,
activating microphones, while
pretending
to be hummingbirds,

rubythroats, with
gossamer-fast
wings.

open-hearth policy

speculate on the nature of triumphant spitfires.
besmirch the good nature of the pekinese.
the ungodly persist in their ungodliness
and the nature of the ecological sanctity of
the small press remains in flux, but,
mercifully, intact.
**
i once stood outside an apartment window
and watched a cute red-haired boy
jerk off. he used corn oil to lubricate
his big shiny dick, and, when he came,
he sure spurted a heck of a lot of cum.
**
the lost, the sad, the lonely,
wander from place to place, person
to person,
hoping for a cessation of pain.
**
a flounder, lying on the bottom of the
sea, looks upward with both of its eyes,
eyes which are, in fact, sitting
on the top of its face.
the flounder is indeed a strange-looking fish, its
face twisted, kind of like
a figure in a picasso painting,
the waves splashing high overhead,
the sunlight a turgid beam
of radiant delight.
**
wonder whatever happened to that
good-looking red-haired boy who used
to jerk off in front of his window.
one day his apartment was simply
empty. he was gone,
and whoever moved in after him,
remains a big fat
blank.

rope and tiger

"the lion's gate opened, and a kitten
emerged. then the kitten changed into
a sexy naked big-dicked teenage boy
who jerked off and spurted cum
and then his genitals changed
into a furry little kitten, mewing
plaintively."
**
"dude!! gross!! i fuckin' HATE that
dream!!!"
**
"me, too," said the young man
who had dreamed it.
**
both parts of this conversation
were sexy sophomore college boys.
it was late at night.
they were roommates.
they had been smoking grass,
and talking for close to 3 hours
now. it was 2 a.m.
the sky outside their
5th-floor dormitory window a spatter
of stars, and a half-hearted
wispy half-moon.
**
"dude, you really shouldn't
go dreaming dreams like that.
they might seriously fuck up
your brain!" said
the sexy college sophomore
boy who had just listened
to his roommate tell him
that fucked-up dream.
**
"i didn't want to dream
it," said
the dreamer. "it just

sorta happened."
**

"dude!" said the listener.
"dude!!"
**

"and the weirdest part,"
said the dreamer. "was when
i woke up, i had a hardon
and i'd already spurted
cum all over my belly."
**

"dude!!" said the listener.
**

then both these good-looking
college sophomore boys
smoked a little bit more.
then, kind of like they
knew it was gonna happen,
but didn't really hope for it,
but sorta did,
they took off all their
clothes and climbed into
the bottom bunk and
sucked on each other's dicks
until they spurted their
hot smelly cum into
each other's hot eager mouths.
**

then the two good-looking
college sophomore boys
lay there
naked, their arms wrapped
around each other,
their chests pressed together,
their lips close,
inhaling each other's breath.
**

"weird night, a night when
no one wants to be lonely,"
said the dreamer. then, "no one

wants to have weird dreams,
and then think about 'em,
all alone," he added.
then, more: "i
love ya, man," he added.
**

"dude!" said the listener.
then,
"i love ya, too, dude," he
said,
as a little "post-orgasm" droplet of
cum
dripped from the tip of
each of their big sturdy dicks
and landed silently
amongst the wrinkles of
the white sweaty sheet.

prurient salsa

by the fireplace, the stockings are hung,
and the turtle doves are
sad sacks of feathers.
the crispin accentuation of
evergreen features merely
goes to prove the
slogan that
wintertime can be hell.
**
however, in his room,
on this cold winter day,
the sexy naked big-dicked teenage boy
stands ruminating on
the uncertainties of just
about everything,
except the
sweet succulent joy of orgasm.
the sexy naked big-dicked teenage boy
is gently tugging on his own great
big smooth hot dick,
as he watches the snow falling
outside his window.
the sexy naked big-dicked teenage boy
has a candy cane in his mouth,
and he is sucking on
it as he tugs on his hard thick dick.
the snow falls.
he sucks on his candy cane.
he tugs on his dick some more.
he begins spurting cum,
and his eyes close tight
as he spurts and spurts and
spurts hot
gooey cum.
then,
the snow falling outside his window,
the candy cane wet and slippery
and sugary in his mouth,

the sexy naked big-dicked teenage boy
kind of whimpers.
it's almost a sob,
but not quite
that serious.

hairy knuckles

i know how people feel.
you want empathy?
well, i'm lousy with empathy.
i know what people like.
i know what people don't like.
and yet, i continue to give
them what they don't like.
and i know they don't like it.
and yet i give it to them anyway.
does that make me an anti-social brat?
or does that make me someone who sticks by
his artistic standards?
makes me a person of artistic integrity?
well, everything in this world isn't
related to the relationship of one's
art to one's personal relationships,
now is it? sometimes it comes
down to just people talking with
people, and no art to stand
in the middle of that communication.
sometimes the communication is
just pure communication, person
to person, talk to talk.
but, even then, i can feel
them backing away, because
i know what they feel.
i'm really quite empathetic.
i understand what they're
feeling, what they're thinking.
i can see the cringe.
feel the uneasiness.
feel the queasy sense
of uh-oh. their twitchy
eyes, my twitchy smile.
i'm sorry we're all
so uncomfortable here.
well, only just a little
bit sorry.

and they know i'm
not REALLY sorry, either.
nobody here's an idiot.
anyone could see that.
we're all just too damn
smart.

big-boned

waddling on the brink of obscurity,
the sexy college sophomore boy
decides if fame has eluded him so far,
the only thing to do
is strip naked and run on the university
sidewalks until he is stopped by
the proper authorities.
as a result of the act of running naked
and getting stopped by
the proper authorities, he's sure
he'll get all kinds of
attention. and that he will be
obscure no more.
so, on a warm sunny day,
the sexy college sophomore boy
strips naked and begins
his run along the sidewalks, making his
way between the crowds of giggling students
trying to make their way to class.
he is noticed, and soon
he is picked up by the cops.
they make him get dressed and charge
him with indecent exposure and
tell him he'll be appearing
in court for sentencing.
he's set free on
his own promise to show up
in court, and not to goddamn run
naked no goddamn more.
back in his dorm room,
his roommate says to him
"what a jerk you are! what
an idiot! why the fuck did
you run naked across campus?"
the sexy college sophomore boy
replies to his not-so-sexy
college sophomore boy roommate:
"i wanted to be famous."

this sounds so funny
that both of them burst
into laughter, and,
from that moment on,
what had been a rather shaky relationship,
at best,
turns into a heartfelt friendship,
that stands the test of time,
a court date,
a fine of $500 and community service,
and
what soon quickly becomes
the
road to obscurity, after all.

green green green

while crunching on a celery stick
with his big white teeth,
the sexy naked big-dicked teenage boy
watched himself in
the big mirror that was mounted
on the back of his bedroom door.
the sexy naked big-dicked teenage boy
looked good,
lean, lithe, sinewy, athletic,
standing in front of that mirror,
crunching away on that celery stick.
in fact,
he looked the pink of health.
his big thick dick was
hard as a rock.
his jaw muscles were tight
and firm and made his
jaws look especially sexy
and rugged
as they worked with his
teeth and tongue and
throat all nicely coordinated
to finish off that
nice crunchy celery stick.
in fact,
the sexy naked big-dicked teenage boy
looked so good
that he took it for granted
that he'd always look this good,
took it for granted that
he'd never get old.
took it for granted that
his big thick dick would
always work this well
and stay this hard
for whatever he wanted
it to stay hard for.
the sexy naked big-dicked teenage boy

stands there crunching the heck
out of that celery stick.
a moment in time.
that, by all rights,
should just
go on
forever.

do not leave chewing gum in water fountain

when the warden on duty passed the empty ketchup bottle,
the day was already pretty much a wildebeest of molasses.
he'd just seen sexy jake and jake's 4 sexy pals suck each
other off. he'd seen the sky turn from blue to black
to pink, and then back to blue. he'd seen earthlings
outnumbered by extraterrestrials 3 to 1, and,
when the next fleet of spaceships arrived,
it was only 2 p.m.
**
the warden turned around, picked up the
ketchup bottle, removed the lid, and
sniffed inside. smelled like
ketchup, with just a hint of
malfeasance. when he sure no one was
looking, he slipped it into his
pocket, and everyone just thought
he was walking around with a hardon.
**
later that night, when he was
off-duty,
the french fries were the best
he'd ever had.

bloom

phone rings.
i pick up. it's darwin on the phone.
"darwin" says darwin.
"er" i say.
"darwin" says darwin.
"yeah?" i say.
"darwin" says darwin.
"pity about the dinosaurs" i say.
"darwin" says darwin.
"pity about the passenger pigeons" i say.
"darwin" says darwin.
"all those little galapagos finches --
they're just so darn cute" i say.
"darwin" says darwin.
i think by now darwin is crying.
"their beaks" i say, "their lovely little beaks
are just so, well, so useful, so practical."
by now i'm crying too.
"darwin" says darwin.
"good-bye" i say.
"darwin" says darwin.
i hear the "click" on the other end.
i hang up.
i'm very sad, but kinda, well, not sad at
all. then i have
pancakes for breakfast. with blueberries.
genetic miracles. bigger than they ever were
before.

just flirting

every once in a while, i fall out of love with
the tidy little life i'm living.
i fall out of love with a clean house.
with clean bathrooms.
with washing dishes and leaving the
kitchen squeaky clean.
everything orderly and in its proper place.
filing system working great.
every once in a while, i think i crave
squalor.
filth. chaos.
disarray. maybe even...
depravity.
or so i say now...
but, in reality
all that filth and chaos
stuff scares me
shitless. kinda.
mostly.
still, though,
standing at the sink,
washing the dishes,
everything so quiet,
and pleasant,
and good,
i think i understand
your average every-day serial
killer,
and what leads him there,
to
where he
went.

bye

over the years,
i have met a lot of people, and
some of them i became friendly with.
and some of those
i have abandoned,
dropped,
ignored,
or otherwise
banished through neglect.
**
i let them fade away
because within me
the main feeling
i began to feel about
them was
disinterest,
dislike,
disgust,
overfamiliarity:
a general feeling
of "ich."
**
after i dismissed
them, i was
glad to never see
them again.
**
i say this
as if i am proud
of myself, yet truly
i am not.
**
it makes me sound
cold, merciless, snobby.
**
actually, i have this recurring
dream in which my heart has
been removed and then replaced

by a little ice cube.
somehow the ice cube never melts, and
yet it keeps on getting
smaller and smaller. soon, it's
so little, it's hardly even worth
bothering about: an afterthought of
an afterthought, beating so very quietly,
it barely makes a sound.

cheap shot

so i'm having a dream about
a guy i had a big crush on back in
high school, a basketball player
named David.
**
i am just sliding my tongue
down his long lean belly
toward his smooth lovely
cock, when, there IS A KNOCK
ON THE DOOR TO OUR APARTMENT!!! (in
the dream, we are both still 18, and
we seem to have just gotten
an apartment together, all of which is
just fine by me!!) well, after
the knock on our door,
an exaggerated look of panic appears
on David's handsome face.
we both get dressed in a hurry, he
opens the door, and,
yes indeed, his parents are
standing there right outside
in the hallway. he sputters,
says "come in", or "just a minute"
or something like that. meanwhile,
the apartment adjoining ours has
mysteriously sprouted a door
that leads directly into our
bathroom, and people from
the apartment next door are
looking into our own apartment with a great
deal of curiosity and disapproval
written all over their smug prying faces.
somehow, we send his parents
away for a while. we close
and lock the mysteriously-
appeared door that leads
into our bathroom from the
adjoining apartment. David and i are

again naked, kissing, fondling,
again deliriously happy that
FINALLY WE GET TO HAVE SEX!!!
i have never wanted
anything so much in my entire life.
we spent our entire senior year
of high school in denial about our love for
each other, but now we've moved in together,
told each other how we feel, and now WE FINALLY
GET TO HAVE SEX!!!
he is my first love, my
first lust. i could just
eat him up. then, the curtains on the
windows glide open. people are milling
around outside our apartment. he is
jittery, unhappy, unwilling;
this is not to be: there
will be no sex with him tonight. i wake up,
sad, frustrated, angry. that which
never happened, never gets to.
not even in a dream.
**

36 years was a long time ago,
but to have it again within my
grasp, and, then have it snatched away--
that just seems
cruel, unbearable, and downright mean.
**

whoever said "a man's reach should
exceed his grasp" had obviously
never dreamed about David, 6'5", 9".

always look twice before crossing the street

even if i'm feeling really really bad,
i must write with a certain level of sanity.
otherwise, i might be misunderstood.
or not understood at all.
my words adrift like milkweed fluff, dandelion
seeds. even if i am feeling really really
insane, i must write as if i'm at least sane
enough to communicate. mustn't i?
**
first of all, i recommend that you
never write anything about writing.
i recommend that you don't write
poems about writing poems.
i recommend that you don't write
books about writing books.
just don't do any of
that stuff, okay? sheesh.
**
several days in a row, in the
locker room, while i am doing
sit-ups on the mat, there is
this incredibly sexy boy
who takes off his work-out
clothes and goes and takes a
shower and comes back to
his locker and gets dressed.
this all happens right across
from where i am doing sit-ups.
he's approximately 12 feet
away from me while he's
undressing. the shower
is far away, hundreds
of feet away, but then he
returns from the
shower and he finishes
toweling himself off and
he gets
dressed, and he is

wildly hugely sexy
with a big thick spectacular
dick.
**
i get a little crazy when
i see stuff like that,
but i'm so well behaved,
it almost makes me sick.

slower, yes, much more slowly than that

i thought nothing of squirrel's breath coming out of
my ears as i stood
naked in the dark in the hallway outside
the bedroom of my sexy college roommate,
him a swimmer on the swimteam, sexy guy,
i was wild about him, delirious nearly,
me just a skinny blond guy majoring
in biology and minoring in english,
him majoring in electrical engineering
and understanding that manly discipline,
such a sweet hot guy, with such
a sweet hot body, and on the
college swimteam to boot!, how
i stood it standing there
outside his bedroom door,
me naked, it is dark,
i'm pretty sure he's not
asleep yet, i think
thoughts about crawling
into bed with him, but
i'm sure he's straight,
and i'm not actually
sure yet i'm gay, but
as i stand naked there
in the dark outside
his bedroom, everything
is real dark and real
quiet and the squirrel's
breath coming out of my
ears is making a slow
hissing sound, torrid,
lost,
stranded.

good B.J. (conceptually speaking)

i like controversial art, but
i hate controversy.
i have written stuff
on bathroom walls, and i like
to read stuff that others have written
on bathroom walls.
i like seeing outrageous stuff
put on a wall, or on paper,
or made into a 3-dimensional work
of art,
or spread across a computer screen.
but i don't want to stand face-to-face
against somebody and scream
my words at them while they
disagree with what i say.
i don't want to see
the whites of their eyes,
i don't want to be able
to focus first-hand on
the pinks of their tongues.
i'd rather they read what
i have written, read
it while hundreds of
miles away from me,
and keep that distance.
does this make me
cowardly (probably), or
is it just a way for
me to maintain
my artistic objectivity?
(whatever that is.)
geee, i like controversial art,
but i hate controversy.
you know, i would never kill a pig
myself,
but i sure love to eat pork.
there's dirty work,
and then there's DIRTY work.

i love to read about two
cute teenage boys fucking each
other up the ass,
i love to see images of two
cute teenage boys fucking
each other up the ass,
but do i want to defend
that kind of art
face-to-face
to those who hate
it and who are offended
by it?
no.
but it's fun to
imagine the offended smoldering,
and sweating,
and getting their hackles up.
it's fun to have fun.
and tougher to explain why
fun IS fun.
knowing that people
look at art and
get mad
because of what they are
seeing,
is fun for me.
having somebody standing
in my face, yelling,
um,
not so much.
some acorns grow into great big oak
trees, but most of those
acorns just rot,
or get eaten by squirrels,
before anything can happen.
all those hot sexy teenage boys
spurting all that hot gooey cum,
most of it never seen,
most of it just
goes quietly down

a bathtub drain,
never bothers a soul,
not even
a bird gets to see it
go.

don't put turnips in your pockets

i found my old high-school locker in the woods.
it smelled liked greasy metal.
i just kind of stumbled onto it.
i knew right away it was my old high-school locker.
i'm not really sure exactly how i knew it
was my old high-school locker at first sight.
but i just knew.
it was gray, and had "breathing slots" near the
top.
then, of course, my old latin iii textbook with
my name in it proved beyond all doubt that
this was the locker that had belonged to me.
there was a gooey layer all over everything.
from the smell, i realized it was cum.
at first i thought it was my own cum,
spurted when i was a teenage boy.
and then i decided it was the cum
of lots of different teenage boys,
my own included,
spurted onto the outside of my locker,
and
into my locker,
just absolutely
drenching everything in my locker
with teenage-boy cum.
the smell of all that teenage-boy cum,
that,
and the smell of greasy metal,
made
me feel strange.
the latin iii textbook felt kind of tacky.
i'm 59 years old now.
it was a quiet day in the woods,
not even a breeze,
just the sound of pine needles crackling
under foot,
and that discovery of my old high-school locker.
actually,

i found the whole thing pretty exciting,
the smell of all that teenage-boy cum,
the general oddness of the situation.
when i sat down and started translating the latin,
i was surprised just how much latin i remembered,
more than you'd think, and
surprised by just
how much metal could smell like grease,
how much teenage-boy cum could smell like greasy metal,
and how
long it took
to read one line of vergil,
while
the oozing of time burned the inside of
my throat.

the sidewalk

overheard by me:
**
"I just can't get over the fact that
I never even talked to that
girl, and she still ended up
in my bed."
**
these words were spoken by
one cute guy to another cute guy.
these two guys were just
walking by on the sidewalk,
coming toward me,
and i happened to overhear what
they were saying.
**
i love overhearing pieces of conversations.
**
"I just can't get over the fact that
I never even talked to that
girl, and she still ended up
in my bed."
**
spoken soft, easy, no hint
of bragging, just, sharing, kind of,
marvelling.
**
i'm 62 years old.
those two guys were probably
around 20 or so.
they seemed to be having a
real moment of sharing,
a real heart-to-heart moment.
**
i don't know how long it's
been since i've had
a good cry.
**
i sort of felt like it then,

though.
**

i love overhearing pieces
of conversations.
it's almost like hearing people
share their poems.
**

it's almost like i was
that girl, in that
warm marvellous
bed, my arms around,
well,
just everything.

prick

the taters are on the couch, and
it's raining outside, and the
taters are blended into a position
between a snuggle and a doze,
and the tv is on, and the light
is soft and muted and the
sound isn't harsh, but
it isn't pretty either.
**
outside, the taters's skinny
sexy son is hidden in the
bushes outside the
den window watching the
taters sleep/snuggle in front
of their tv
on their couch.
**
soon, the taters's son is taking
off his shirt and feeling
the cool drops of rain on
his back and shoulders. it
is a hot night, and air
conditioners everywhere
in the neighborhood are
purring like cats.
**
soon, the taters's son takes off
his pants and is kneeling there
on the ground outside the taters's
den window while his parents
the taters are
sleeping/snuggling on the couch
in front of the tv.
**
the rain falls gently on his
naked back and shoulders and
legs; his underpants are tight
and white and under their

clinging dampness is revealed
quite sharply the outlines
of the big hard smooth erect dick
and smooth tight balls of
the taters's mostly-naked
son as he crouches outside
the taters's window in the warm
summer rain.
**

his parents the taters whimper
softly and move slightly closer
to each other on the couch.
the taters's skinny sexy big-dicked son
begins to cry. he stands up
wearing only his revealing underpants
and his tennis shoes and he walks
into the middle of the backyard.
he stands there staring up into
the rain, crying, thinking
about the possibility of his
own suicide and about jerking off
in the rain, and he strips off
his wet underpants and stands
there in the middle of the
backyard jerking off in the
warm summer rain; when he spurts
cum, it falls hot and slimy
like slugs mating on the wet grass.
**

then he puts his wet underpants
back on, returns to the
window outside the den
with the tv in it, retrieves
his wet shirt and wet pants and puts
them back on with considerable
difficulty. he stands there
outside the den window looking
at his parents the taters as they
snuggle/sleep in front of the
tv on the couch in the

den in the wet darkness
of the hot summer night.
**

the taters's smooth sexy
son seriously considers
methods by which suicide
might be accomplished, then
goes to the back door,
unlocks it quietly,
enters the kitchen,
takes off his shoes,
leaves them by the door,
and grabs a handful of
meat from the refrigerator.
he stands there in the
middle of the kitchen
gnawing at the handful
of meat, and he growls
and growls and growls,
but nobody
wakes up.

sparklers on the 4th of july

i'm just an old guy,
drifting into old age.
i'm thinking
back to
when i was young and sexy,
and now,
well,
i just grin at my innocence,
and smirk at my naievete.
**
all those sexy
young men today, though,
all those sexy young men with
their big sturdy dicks
and their wild eyes
and their wild dreams
of sexually representing
themselves to the world,
are still a fascinating
breed, a world unto themselves,
happy slaves to their big
beautiful erections,
fountains of cum,
their sexual scent of cum-musk
a heady and enticing brew.
they walk around
with their tight sexy sex pants
showing off what they've got,
they
feel whole and
alive
and
important.
**
me, old, and
dwindling,
and
my memory's still

pretty good though,
real good, in fact,
in some ways,
just too damn
good.

open window

on some pornographic websites, i see photographs of
guys pissing on each other.
these guys are cute young men (often
VERY cute young men),
and they seem to be having such fun pissing
on each other,
there's this look in their eyes,
kinda giddy, kinda wild, actually,
and they certainly give the impression
that pissing on each other is just
another way of having good clean sexual fun.
**
once, a long time ago,
i was in bed with a guy who asked
me to piss in his mouth.
so i did.
turns out i squirted so much pee into
his mouth that
he wasn't able to swallow it all
and
some of it dribbled down his chin,
and it was, well, sorta icky.
i was drunk and stoned at the time,
and i didn't think he was all that attractive,
and, well,
i guess the whole experience
wasn't very much fun for me,
and i kinda got the feeling
it didn't turn out to be so much
fun for him, either, since
i pissed such an unexpectedly
large volume of pee into
his mouth.
**
but the sexy good-looking naked
young men pissing on
each other in those
website photos sure look

like they're having fun.
**

sometimes i think
back about various things
i've done during my life.
various sexual things.
i'm sure most people
do that, from time to time.
think back over things
they've done.
things they wish they'd
done.
things that they'd have done
if they'd been given the chance.
things they might
still do,
perhaps in the
bathtub, so the
mattress won't get
wet.
**

not that a wet mattress is
the worst thing
in the world.
**

still, though,
i think
ya know what i mean.

combo

the sexy naked big-dicked teenage boy was
eating a sandwich, savoring
his favorite part, the thick rich layer of mayonnaise.
his mayonnaise-induced euphoria lasted only a short while,
however, and then another species went extinct. but, just
a couple minutes after that,
a previously unknown species was discovered somewhere
in the lushness of the tropics. so he figured that made it okay.
**

the sexy naked big-dicked teenage boy
went back to eating his mayonnaise-slathered
sandwich. everything else was secondary: meat,
tomato, cheese. the mayonnaise was the
important element, the most desired flavor.
**

that night,
the sexy naked big-dicked teenage boy
heard on the news that
at least TWO HUNDRED brand-new deep-sea species
had just been discovered.
TWO HUNDRED!
this news made him smile.
he liked the idea that the earth was teeming
with life, all kinds of it.
**

lying naked in bed that night, on his back,
all the covers thrown off,
jerking off,
the sexy naked big-dicked teenage boy
smeared mayonnaise on his dick
and spurted cum all over his chest and
belly. he could practically feel
all those little spermatozoans wriggling
around on his skin, trapped in the
blobs of mayo that still clung to his
fingers and dick shaft. he could
sense their
wriggliness wane, however,

and quickly accepted the
knowledge that today
was their day
to die.

trouser trout

the broom sedge on the hill moves wildly
to and fro
as flocks of black birds fly over the
flexing shafts of orange.
it is autumn.
the day is warm. also on the hill, very
near its top, and
amongst the wind-whipped shafts of
broom sedge, two sexy naked young men
lie atop
an old musty dark green blanket.
they are
lying on their sides, facing
one another,
and their
hands are all over each
other -- nipples, butts, dicks, balls --
they can't keep their hands off
of each other as
the wind whips the
broom sedge, and
up above, black birds
drift in the wind.
autumn is
in the air, and when the
young men start spurting
cum, the broom sedge moves
to and fro, the black
birds drift above,
and the lips of
the two sexy naked young men
are open wide, sucking in air
as if they couldn't get enough of it,
the flavor of the autumn air,
the wind whipping all around, black
birds drifting above, and, down
below, this blanket, these two
naked young men, their

cum on each other's bellies,
their eyes shiny like dirty books,
the beautiful ones, with
really naughty covers.

individual rights in the time of crisis

at the height of
the midatlantic drift,
the smiling mermen began pairing
off with one another most
charmingly,
and, attesting eagerly to their
masculine aquatic beauty,
gradually finding solace in
the soft fronds of kelp,
hundreds of yards long,
drifting like wedding gowns,
but even better.
**
when it began to rain
on the sexy lonely naked teenage boy,
he cussed everything he could
think of,
and the trees around him blushed,
and dropped all their leaves.
autumn had never in the history
of time been known to fall
this fast or
this hard.
**
while the mermen were fucking
each other with their mysteriously aligned
but highly functioning genitalia,
the sexy lonely naked teenage boy
began raking up all the fallen leaves,
and sweeping them out
to sea. it wasn't a pretty solution
to the problem, but sometimes elegance
is the first thing to go.

dinner time yet

in this phase of your life, you are a
beautiful sexy naked smoldering big-dicked big-eyed boy.
today, you
throw yourself down on your bed and weep.
you are sad, you are disillusioned. you are sick
with nebulous and generalized grief.
you are a
beautiful sexy naked smoldering big-dicked big-eyed boy
and yet,
yet, you are all of this unhappiness.
you are miserable.
your beauty is not enough.
it hasn't helped you in any way that has
brought you meaning, peace, understanding,
tranquility.
you want to die.
you lie on your bed weeping.
you, at this phase of your life,
a beautiful sexy naked smoldering big-dicked big-eyed boy,
unhappy and sick at heart.
**
years later,
you are a little old man.
you think back to how beautiful you were.
you have the photographs to prove it.
a little old man now,
you are constantly sad,
and wonder what it all meant,
life, your former beauty,
your ignorance of how everything
worked, or could be made to work,
how everything just kind of slipped
by, and left you here, now,
a little old man,
achy, finicky,
and
bewildered.
**

you are now flecks of debris
adrift in the winter wind.
it is snowing.
the sky is quite gray.
**
pottery lasts for thousands
of years.
i like the vases that have
drawings of sexy naked greek young
men running races together,
their dicks
flopping saucily, up, and down.

rounds

oh it's just a matter of time until
the peaches fall from their trees and
into the tooth-studded jaws of the slick red foxes who
wait so restlessly below, their
eyes umber fire, tongues licking their
feral lips with long delicate
slick wet pinknesses.
the rooftops, hot ruddy terra cotta
tiles in the 110 degrees
Fahrenheit summer
heat, holes in the
golf courses plugged
up with the most obscene
of all possible debris--
hankies soaked with
the cum of
svelte naked young men,
their penis-tips still warm
and smeary with the open
hostility of their
own pent-up goo.
clicking cameras sometimes
catch all the action, but,
only rarely,
the steam.

flavor

oh yes, it is indeed possible that Zac Efron is the
sexiest most handsome young man on the planet.
yes, it is indeed possible that every young gay boy,
that every gay teenage boy,
that every gay young man, that every gay 30-something
man, that every gay middle-age man, and that every gay old man
on the planet
who has ever seen even one photograph of Zac Efron or
who has seen Zac Efron act in even one movie
entertains the thought of gently licking
Zac Efron's balls.
and yes,
it is indeed possible that ANYbody on the planet
with any sense knows that
Zac Efron, yes, KNOWS
that Zac Efron is almost excruciatingly attractive,
knows
that Zac Efron is handsome beyond almost
all standard measures of handsomeness,
knows that Zac Efron is
sexy way beyond almost all measures of sexiness.
gay males, straight females, and no doubt
bi males and bi females, too, think
about Zac Efron in terms that are sexual.
some straight males, too, yes males
who know that they are heterosexual, perhaps
nonetheless find themselves thinking
about Zac Efron in terms that are
frankly, sexual. in fact, some heterosexual
males are no doubt disturbed to wake
up in the middle of the night
fresh from a dream involving an imagined Zac Efron
movie and a Zac Efron scene
is which there is full frontal nudity of
a Zac Efron kind.
Most disturbing of all, to these kind
of men, is that whenever they spell
his name, they always spell it
right.

patterns on the landscape of dreams

the certainty of punishment was unbearable.
the fact that there was never forgiveness was
beyond all understanding.
and what had this gentle sexy teenage boy, done, really,
to warrant such treatment? beyond being
gentle, and sexy, that is. what had
this gentle sexy teenage boy DONE to
bring this abuse upon himself?
and why was his father still beating him? STILL beating him?
after all these years.
didn't most fathers stop "spanking" their sons
when their sons got older?
not this father, though.
now, this gentle sexy teenage boy
was bent over the edge of his bed,
his pants and underpants down around
his ankles, his shirt off, while
his father flailed away at him,
with leather belt, on
this gentle sexy teenage boy's naked
back and butt and backs of legs.
and, then, it was over.
his father stormed out of the room.
the gentle sexy teenage boy lay
there over the bed a few moments
more, the red welts left
by the beating stinging and
burning and throbbing.
he pulled up his
underpants, pulled up
his pants, put on a shirt. then,
the gentle sexy teenage boy
looked out the window, looked far
off into the distant woods,
he could see the leaves
shimmering like
pieces of emeralds,
before they're cut, faceted,

sold. he understood there's
quite a market for
emeralds, in some
parts of the world.
men dressed in flowing
skirts, mustaches always
neatly trimmed.

peaches and pears

the classical study of study
requires a nude model,
preferably a sexy naked teenage boy,
and he stands there
contrapposto (his weight on
one foot) and he's looking dreamily
off into space,
and his lips are lightly parted,
and you can see his
tongue dancing around
in there, easy to ignore that,
though, easier than
his big smooth dick,
for he has
one erection after the other,
as the hour goes on,
but time
stops, and
thrusts itself right
in your face.

smackers and crackers

when using the special anti-clogging apparatus,
it is important to make the insertion
technique as smooth as possible.
when done smoothly, insertion of
the special anti-clogging apparatus
can seem like a spring day, breezy,
with a nice bright sun high
above the fluffy white clouds.
the special anti-clogging apparatus is
competently and capably designed for
easy insertion. still, if it
is forced, there can be
objectionality. whenever
the sexy naked big-dicked teenage boy
is practicing the use of
the special anti-clogging apparatus,
he always takes it
very slow. then, when
the special anti-clogging apparatus
is perfectly in place,
the sexy naked big-dicked teenage boy
manipulates it gently, carefully,
and, before too long,
the sexy naked big-dicked teenage boy
is quite satisfied. it is then
and only then that
the sexy naked big-dicked teenage boy
feels capable and ready to demonstrate
the use
of the special anti-clogging apparatus,
and licensure is soon to follow.
the license he receives is really
quite lovely: framed, on a wall
in a quiet and well-kept office,
it is truly a thing of beauty.

twice that many

squash for dinner, and squash for lunch.
squash squash squash.
harbinger of autumn.
prelude to halloween.
taste buds awash in their softness, their delicate stringiness.
gentle fibres caressing tongue and
insides of cheeks and back of
soft pink throat. thus sits
the sexy gentle country boy in
his seat at the kitchen table
eating the squash that he
has prepared for himself
from his own garden
out behind the old house
in which he has sequestered himself
for the better part of a year.
dropped out of college.
dropped out of as much of life as possible.
lucky to have this house, and this land,
left to him by loving
grandmother in
her will at just about
the time he made the decision to
drop out of
college and drop out of life and, well,
drop out of just about everything for a while.
now,
sitting at his little table all alone
eating a variety of squash for dinner,
he
considers
decisions he's made,
decisions he's about to make,
decisions he'll never make because
he's just so
entrenched here,
all alone,
as

he rises from the table,
the sexy gentle country boy is naked
as usual,
he spends as much time as
possible naked,
he's really quite beautiful,
tousled blond hair and
tanned all over
and lean muscles under tight
skin
his big thick dick
hanging over his nice set of balls.
he goes to the sink
and washes the plate and
the pans he used to prepare
the squash.
there is squash
skin on the countertops,
squash skin at the edge of the sink.
the squash skin is knobby and multi-colored.
he likes the way it
just lies there
and
waits for him to
do something about it,
which he most certainly will,
when the spirit moves him,
when the time just seems
right.

too too

the gratitude of a nation was nearly inexpressible
as it contemplated
the sacrifices
of its gay leaders,
their struggle and their
demands and their
explanations.
oh how the nation
was grateful to its gay leaders,
oh how the nation
loved them and embraced them
and wished them well. "we love
the homosexuals," said the nation.
"we just adore them!"
**
no sarcasm intended.
**
really.

spread 'em

again, the exalted one has declared himself to
be the absolute best, and, once
again, no one is disputing.
of course,
the exalted one is hot-looking, sexy,
physically stunning, and big-dicked. also,
he has a great face, with a wonderful smile.
he has a great personality, too.
not a mean bone in his body. people always
love him when they meet him. and those that
get to have sex with him, always
enjoy the experience. everybody always cums.
with a smile on their face, and
an ecstatic pleasurable moan.
if only the exalted one wouldn't
persist in referring to himself
in that manner, though. yes,
he really does refer to himself
as "the exalted one." it's
kind of off-putting. it would,
in fact, be downright annoying,
if it weren't so goddamn true.

poe, hawthorne, and melville -- sir!

a sunny spot in the middle of
the woods: there's a stream nearby.
it's making honest-to-gosh babbling sounds
as the sexy naked big-dicked ROTC cadet and
the sexy naked big-dicked american lit major
sit talking to each other.
"here, have some more weed," says
the sexy naked big-dicked ROTC cadet as he
passes the joint over to the
sexy naked big-dicked american lit major.
the sexy naked big-dicked american lit major inhales
deeply. "i'd like to suck you off now," he says.
one thing quickly leads to another,
and, very soon,
each of them freshly sucked off by the other, they
lie there side by side, still naked,
looking up into the big blue sky.
"your cum tastes like old books,"
the sexy naked big-dicked ROTC cadet says to the
sexy naked big-dicked american lit major.
"well, your cum tastes like gunpowder,"
the sexy naked big-dicked american lit major says
to the sexy naked big-dicked ROTC cadet.
"since when have you ever eaten an old book?" says
the sexy naked big-dicked american lit major.
"and since when have you ever eaten gunpowder?"
says the sexy naked big-dicked ROTC cadet.
a moment of silence ensues.
"i guess this means we're in love,
doesn't it?" says the sexy naked big-dicked
american lit major.
"that we are," says the
sexy naked big-dicked ROTC cadet.
"good," says the sexy naked big-dicked
american lit major.
"real good," says the sexy naked big-dicked
ROTC cadet.
when the sun starts to set,

they embrace each other, and
hang on tight, lilac and vinegar,
oil and water, hot like
moon-lit steam.

cranberry juice spritzer with twist of vodka pete, please

the swig and swagger of broad back and
big floppy cock and sexy tiny-nippled
chest--these were the things he noticed
as he sat, benched, eyes fixed
and roaming like lust-starved bulls,
targeting for zoom-in close the
great faces and naked
well-delineated-striated-style-
skinny-smooth-
tongue-tip-tasty
bellies
of sexy near-naked young men,
the cries of seabirds and the aerial
drift of cloud surfaces the pandemonium
center, the source of silent guttural
growls emanating from close to the back
of his throat, but, more likely,
from the very center of the
longing center that spread from
his chest-central, and crept on
down toward the realm of his
genital cockwad-minded ballsiness,
his heart going thump thump thump,
the sounds lost in the seascape
of bending skin and flexing muscle,
sinew tight but yet well lubricated
thoughts racing and flexing as only found
in the knees and the elbows anatomy
a shrill song of precision run amuck
on the landscape and
quagmire of neo-spunky and
quick-fingered transcendent desire.

luna lunar lunatic

the miracle of trips to the moon
is that no one ever screams "faggot"
because everyone is too interested
in the science and engineering and wonderment
of it all --
though
i do wonder if any faggot has ever
walked on the moon.
or if any faggot has ever orbited
the moon.
or if any faggot has ever had
a "wet dream" and spurted cum
while asleep and being monitored
by those electrodes that do
that kind of monitoring while
astronauts are asleep in space.
i'm guessing that the monitors
record a high level of
electrical activity during
an orgasm. while the
astronaut sleeps, he
sprouts a woody and
has a dream and spurts
cum. what does the guy
who's looking at the monitor
output down on earth think?
does that monitor guy
know what the
astronaut is dreaming?
of course not, the monitor
guy just
sees the "orgasm" spike,
and grins. nobody down
there knows if the
astronaut is dreaming
of a guy or a girl when
he spurts that cum.
faggotry in outer space

is probably only limited
to dream time anyway--
anything that goes on
in the space ship itself,
you'd think we'd know about
it by now. you'd think.

generic cough syrup

eat all those salads, but
some day you're gonna die.
take all yer vitamins, but
some day you're gonna die.
do your running and walking exercises regularly, but
some day you're gonna die.
**
drink alcohol and smoke cigarettes
and take drugs and have wild
promiscuous sex, and guess
what,
someday you're gonna die.
drive yer car wildly and badly,
and some day you're gonna
die.
**
timing is the issue, i think here.
odds and statistics. how long
you have
until you die is somewhat
in your hands. somewhat.
**
the particular rub is: you decide
to go the healthy healthy healthy
route, and you eat right and
drink right and exercise right,
and a tree falls on your
house with you in it and
smashes you to death
on your 45th birthday while
you're eating a tofu & bean-sprout sandwich.
**
every day's a crap shoot.
every day's a gift, a curse,
a blessing.
the odds for most
of us are that we're gonna
survive today and go

on to the next one. and yet...
ya never know. the odds
are pretty good, though, that
you'll still be around tomorrow.
and yet...
and yet...
and goddamn fucking yet.

how platonic

the resulting correspondence spurred him into action.
oh there was no doubt about it: he was in love
with his new pen-pal. and he was sure his new
pen-pal was just as hot and as sexy a young man
as he himself was. he could picture himself
and his pen-pal together, lying naked
in the woods, side by side, while
in fact he lay all alone by himself
naked on a towel on his belly in a secluded
spot in the woods and wrote page
after page after page after page
to his new pen-pal. this was the
real thing, though, this time.
the real thing. oh sure his pen-pal
was a small-press editor, who lived thousands
of miles away, and who had accepted
and published several of his poems,
but, well, it went
W-A-A-A-A-A-A-A-A-Y-Y-Y beyond
a mere poet-editor relationship. he knew it.
his pen-pal wrote him even when there
were matters totally unrelated to
his poems and to the magazine.
his pen-pal wrote him about
life and milkshakes and chocolate
cookies and the joy of a simple
walk on the beach with the
wind blowing his tousled blond hair
to and fro.
oh yes, he was passionately in love
with his new pen-pal, and often
as he lay there naked on his belly writing
letters to his pen-pal, he would
get an insatiable and tremendous hardon, and
he just lay there, though, on top of it,
feeling the sensation of it against
his taut flat belly, as he wrote
to his pen-pal about matters totally

unrelated to sex. he was fairly
sure his new pen-pal was straight.
which could be a problem. since he
himself was gay and in fact totally
in love with his new pen-pal. but
surely this could all be worked out.
everything didn't have to be about
sex, did it? some things were just
about love. and so he lay there
on his belly his back sweaty
his pink little nipples dripping
sweat his hardon raging, and
he wrote to his pen-pal about
the movie he'd just seen,
the book he was in the middle
of reading, and then,
he kinda broke into tears,
and quickly moved the pages
away, because it was
unseemly to have tear-stains on
letters, no matter what
others may do--that was
just not him. no way.
he was much too smooth
and sophisticated for
something like that.
instead, after he finished
his cry, he added the sentence:
"I'm still in the middle
of the woods and feel a poem
coming on--I'll send it to ya
if I like the way it turns out."
then he wrote "Sincerely yours,"
and put the letter into an
envelope and sealed it up
and he lay there naked
sweaty on his belly
on top of his hardon
and even though it
seemed kind of crass

to bring sex into all
of this, he rubbed
himself against the
soft surface of the
towel until he spurted
cum and, in fact, he
spurted so much cum
that he nearly soaked his
towel, and then he stood
up, looked down, disgusted,
disgruntled, and just thoroughly
thoroughly
vexed.

the neophytes

there was the day that he came home from work
to find milk on the floor, raisins on the ceiling,
bits of toasted bread stuck to the walls.
**

it was of course the first day of spring.
**

and, like any other sexy good-looking big-dicked
young man, he broke down and had a good cry.
**

then came the invasion of the alcohol-induced
lazies; when the telephone rang, it was his
best friend tom. tom was young, sexy,
skinny, and hot. he invited tom right
on over, and then the two of them shared
the alcohol-induced lazies there on
the couch with some porn.
**

things of an intense and highly personal
sexual nature occurred between them.
these sorts of things had occurred before.
but they both continued to downplay the significance.
**

when tom left, the apartment became, once
again, very very quiet. crumbs, once on
the floor, migrated to the walls. lights
flickered.
**

spring. spring. spring. the first
day, the month of june not the longest,
but surely the most supple.

lentils

explicit sex between consenting ponies is a joy to behold.
**

minestrone soup can soothe a cough.
**

sexy young men have been
observed, and filmed, while fucking
the same watermelon.
**

people can think about anything at all while they are
masturbating -- anything at all.
**

you'd be surprised.
**

ok. maybe not.

just the thumbs

cute guys who writhe --
ah cute guys who writhe --
cute guys who really truly WRITHE,
cute guys who roll around naked
on top of the sheets and WRITHE,
really WRITHE, well, they are nothing short of
wonderful. twisting and
turning and rolling and extending
and flexing and well, WRITHING,
god, they are HOT.
cute guys who strip off all
their clothes and writhe,
who roll around naked
and exhibit paroxysms of ecstasy,
who stretch & wriggle & contort themselves
with the pleasure
and passion of being cute and naked
and sexual and alive and sensate
and who writhe and writhe
and writhe as the world
turns slowly: ah, cute guys who
writhe! ah! cute guys who really WRITHE,
and mean it! "contortion" doesn't
begin to describe what they do.
"extreme stretching and flexing" --
that doesn't do it justice either.
"twisting and turning and
displaying themselves passionately and
exuberantly" comes close. but
what these guys do is WRITHE. and
when you see them writhe, you'll
know that what you've seen is writhing, and
you'll know that you want to
see it again. by the way,
people also writhe in
the grips of pain, instead of
in the throes of joy. the
similarity of facial gestures can be

unsettling, and, to some, it is
quite troubling. saints.
ah the tears and screams of the saints.
echoing into the night,
old church walls
shedding their paint.

slurp

the real question
is not why people who are really really unhappy
kill themselves
but why do people who are really really unhappy
keep on living?
i think the answer is complicated and certainly involves
the fear of death but
i think primarily what keeps them
going is hope/belief/optimism that
something good is going to happen.
and that they'll feel better.
the expectation that they won't feel this bad forever.
so they give it another day, and if that's not
enough, they give it
another.
and then yet another. and,
every once in a while, for
most people anyway,
something nice does happen,
a spring day that welcomes you into its
arms instead of excluding you,
great sex (together or alone),
a conversation you thought you'd never have you
do have, and you end up feeling tingly and good
and alive for several days thereafter,
an unexpected sum of money comes into your life,
an old medical problem clears up,
you see a great movie,
you cry for the first time in ages,
you realize you feel sort of even-keel instead
of really awful,
you wake up & feel older & you're glad because
you sure hated the way you felt when you were
younger,
you sit alone staring into blank space & you feel calm,
and without even really thinking about it
in any definite terms at all,
you just settle into the habit

of putting up with the crap and
sucking on the good stuff.

liniment, the panacea of earthly delights

when the grinch stole christmas, trees grew
tall and fat. anderson cooper took off all
his clothes and took a nice hot soapy
shower, and masturbated, too, and
neil patrick harris fantasized
about anderson cooper naked in the
shower. while fantasizing all
alone in his own misty shower,
neil patrick harris
stroked his own nice thick manly dick,
while showering gently, with
lots of shampoo and soap suds,
and,
some of us,
pictured doogie howser, m.d.,
that young doctor naked,
examining me as i lay
on my back naked upon the table.
it seems i have the most
perfect abdominal muscles doogie has
ever seen, and he's simply
transfixed by them.
he palpates them gently,
just to be sure. then,
i receive the finest
blowjob of my life,
doctors know all
those skills, having
studied everything about,
well,
pretty much everything.
the lights go out.
anderson cooper dries off
and lies naked on his back
on his bed, staring into
the eternity.
neil patrick harris
discovers my poems,

and just
has to gasp with
pleasure.
the grinch goes away until
next year,
and the
pine trees are safe once more,
their big fat pine cones looking
tight and green and chloro-phallic--
they are dangerously spikey, though,
among the most
perverse
of all of nature's sexy little tricks.

grandson effectiveness

the sexy naked big-dicked teenage boy
was alone, masturbating in the woods.
he tugged on his dick and tugged
on his dick until he
spurted a big
load of hot cum onto the bark of a tree.
his cum clung there gelatinous
and gooey.
"spurting cum sure is fun," he said.
**
overhead, the leaves of the tree shimmered
in the breeze, and the
sky was bright blue.
**
when the sexy naked big-dicked teenage boy
began putting on his clothes,
his cum was still
oozing down the
tree bark -- what a
slimy trail
it makes
as the leaves
vibrate,
showing first their tops,
then their bottoms.

marigold jelly

a big-dicked blonde boy walked into
a restaurant and
took a
seat by the window.
he had a raging hardon and
it was obvious.
a cockroach crawled up onto
the surface of the table and
started talking to
the big-dicked blonde boy.
"you'd sure look good in an old-fashioned
codpiece," said the cockroach.
"i think you're really built for it," added
the cockroach.
"you really think so?" said
the big-dicked blonde boy, embarrassed by
the attention, yet kind of
flattered, too.
"oh yes indeed i do," said
the cockroach. "you'd look
absolutely great in a codpiece."
"so exactly what is a codpiece?"
said the big-dicked blonde boy.
"it's just an old-fashioned
item of apparel," said the
cockroach, "quite
sexy, too, in a clean overt traditional
kind of way. it's kind of a pouch
for your dick and balls,
gives 'em room, and
shows 'em off
at the same time."
at that moment, a waitress
appeared, and the cockroach went
scurrying away.
the waitress handed the
big-dicked blonde boy

a menu. "what would
you like to drink?" she
asked.
"beer," replied the
big-dicked blonde boy.
the waitress started chuckling.
"got some i.d.?" she asked.
"no," said the big-dicked blonde boy.
"well, sweetie, either you need to order
a soft drink, or i think you'd
better be on your way," she said.
"couldn't you just bring me
a whiskey?"
said the big-dicked blonde boy.
the waitress frowned.
"well, buster, it looks to
me like you'd just better be on
your way," she said to the
big-dicked blonde boy.
he shrugged, stood up,
and walked toward the door.
the cockroach was now sitting on
his collar.
"remember my advice," squeaked
the cockroach, "codpiece
for you -- and i'd make
it a nice soft velvet,
if possible."
"thanks," said
the big-dicked blonde boy,
as he strode off
into the sunlight,
its beams radiant
on his golden hair,
its heat liquid
fire on the front
of his
tight bulging
trousers.

sandpaper quilts

"when navigating the road of life,"
thinks the sexy big-dicked college boy,
"be sure and make time to have plenty
of orgasms." the sexy big-dicked college boy
is on the track team, cross-country,
and as he runs along a narrow footpath
in the middle of the woods, his dick bulges
pleasurably against the pouch
of his jockstrap, and pushes
out the front of his paper-thin
shorts. the sexy big-dicked college boy
is all alone, no one is nearby,
and he thinks of the orgasm he
just had this morning, when
he woke up hard as a rock and jerked off
into his pajama bottoms.
"that was a good orgasm," thinks
the sexy big-dicked college boy.
"and i want lots of those --
big gushy sloppy messy
orgasms where i spurt gallons and
gallons of hot smelly
gooey cum."
the sexy big-dicked college boy
continues running on the narrow
path through the woods,
his dick bulging into the
pouch of his jockstrap,
the front of his tiny
paper-thin little shorts
pushed forward. the birds
are singing, and butterflies
are fluttering about.
he considers stopping to
jerk off, but, then again,
he's got his rhythm going,
so on he goes,
running and running

and running.
**

when he gets back to the locker room
he's in the shower
with all those other beautiful
track team guys. these guys are
all so beautiful
he practically starts
crying.
he doesn't want to
want each and every one of
them like he does. he
wants something
pure, something
non-sexual. something
like friendship, which,
as always, eludes
him once again.
it's not that he's
standoffish. it's just that
he's, well, too "busy".
**

alone in his room
that night,
the sexy big-dicked college boy
who ran alone through the woods
jerks off four separate times,
each time spurting cum like
a swollen firehose.
there ought to be someone
he can talk to, have a
beer with, maybe.
but who?
when?
and
why?

greco-roman wrestling

a car in the rain,
with two people inside it -- it is
a dark and gloomy rain, still daylight,
but fading toward dusk.
the driver is a man. the woman is his wife.
rain falls loudly on
their car,
makes the windows appear slick and
almost slimy.
the windshield wipers are on
full-speed.
**
the car moves on through
the rain, and, as the dusk arrives,
the man says "it'll be nice to
be home." "i'll say," says his wife.
**
it continues raining.
**
the man says something else to his
wife. but the rain is
so loud she can't hear what he said
but she nods agreement anyway.
**
the air in the car
smells wet,
and the rain is
so loud,
the radio is
franz kafka
without the
sardines.

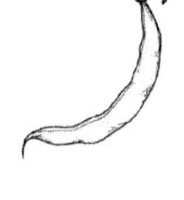

ACKNOWLEDGEMENTS:

The author gratefully acknowledges the following publications where some of these poems first appeared:

And So On...The BareBack Anthology
Assaracus
BareBack Magazine
Carnival Magazine
Censored Poets
Chiron Review
Citizens for Decent Literature
The Commonline Journal
DNA
FUCK!
Gorilla Architecture
Hearing Voices: The BareBack Anthology
Last Train to Noir City
My Favorite Bullet
neo lampshadian outpost
Nerve Cowboy
pLopLop
Poetry Super Highway
Poetz.com
The Thorn Blog
The Quirk
Shy Boys at Home
Underground Voices
Zen Baby
Zygote in my Coffee

ABOUT THE AUTHOR:

CARL MILLER DANIELS lives in the United States. He's not a cowboy, but thinks about them a lot. His poems have appeared in many nice places, including *Assaracus, BareBack Magazine, Chiron Review, Citizens for Decent Literature, DNA, FUCK!, My Favorite Bullet,* and *Zygote in my Coffee*. Daniels has several books in print. Most recently, BareBackPress published his books *Sedimentary Iguana-Land* and *Be Kind to Strangers*. Both are available at the BareBackPress website, as well as at good ole' Amazon, too. Daniels recently turned 65 years old. He and his husband, Jon (aka "the sweetest man in the world"), have been together for over 35 years.

ALSO BY THE AUTHOR

Museum Quality Orgasm

Riot Act

Shy Boys at Home

Gorilla Architecture

Saline

Be Kind to Strangers

Sedimentary Iguana-land

Sedimentary Iguana-Land
Carl Miller Daniels

Sedimentary Iguana-Land, a new book by Carl Miller Daniels. The book consists of rants, musings, lists, poems -- and yes secret forbidden thoughts -- all of which Daniels had scrawled onto 3x5 cards over a period of many years, put into a dusty cardboard box, and kept there in that box, until he said what the heck, and decided to dig them out. Sedimentary Iguana-Land ~ ya ain't seen nothin' like it.

Sedimentary Iguana-Land
$8.50
5.25" x 8"
114 pages
ISBN-13: 978-1926449128
ISBN-10: 1926449126
BISAC: Poetry / General

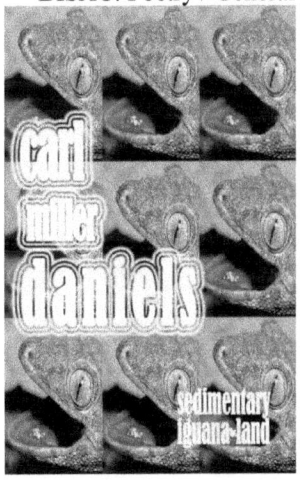

The Human Condition Is A Terminal Illness
Matthew J. Hall

To be human is to come to terms with a repetitive and trying history; an acceptance of the potential beauty and the overiding toxicity of mankind. The Human Condition is a Terminal Illness, pulls individual and societal insecurities out from our collective subconscious in an effort toward analysis and question. More often than not, in the midst of a confused, selfish, self-hating populace, the answers are left wanting.

The Human Condition Is A Terminal Illness
$12.50
5.25" x 8"
140 pages
ISBN-13: 978-1926449111
ISBN-10: 1926449118
BISAC: Poetry / General

A Lark Up The Nose Of Time
Wayne F. Burke

A Lark Up The Nose Of Time, Wayne F. Burke's fourth full length book of poetry, extends from the poet's childhood to present circumstances with accessible and viscerally inclined poems, whimsical and serious by turns...Let the rhythmic language take you on a trip through a harsh poetically-rendered landscape, earthy as well as highly imaginative.

"Not only the most original and authentic collection of poems I've read in years, it's one of the best books period...A masterpiece!" ~ Howard Frank Mosher, author, A STRANGER IN THE KINGDOM, New England Book Award Winner.

A Lark Up The Nose Of Time
$12.50
5.25" x 8"
132 pages
ISBN-13: 978-1926449142
ISBN-10: 1926449142
BISAC: Poetry / General

50 EURO
Karina Bush

Set in the cum-soaked hole of Amsterdam's Red Light District, "50 EURO" is a dark neon glimpse into the activities of those who enter and work these windows.

"Karina Bush is a bright new talent. Keep your eye on her . . . she's one to watch."
~ James Frey, author of "A Million Little Pieces" and "Bright Shiny Morning"

"Karina's work transcends characterization as prose or poetry; she creates her own genre with lyrical flow, masterful form, and unrelenting originality."
~ Christopher Byck, 48th Street Press

50 EURO
$8.50
5.25" x 8"
98 pages
ISBN-13: 978-1926449166
ISBN-10: 1926449169
BISAC: Poetry / General

it will never be this time again
Daman Ferrell Marbut

Poems that walk the line of heartbreak, it will never be this time again is a book of both observation and reconciliation. Damon Ferrell Marbut, with his fourth collection, continues to define the South based on soul rather than geography.

"Reading Damon Ferrell Marbut is like reuniting with an old friend, an intimate experience of reflection where history is freed and the moment is embraced. There is a red-wine warmth which tingles throughout the conversation, and questions cut loose from the burden of answer are broached in whiskey whispers. These poems, though birthed from a life lived with chaos."
~ Matthew J. Hall

it will never be this time again
$8.50
5.25" x 8"
82 pages
ISBN-13: 978-1926449159
ISBN-10: 1926449150
BISAC: Poetry / General

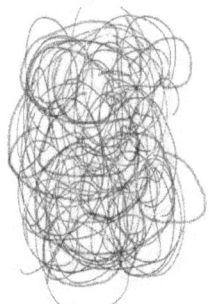

www.barebackpress.com
Hamilton, Canada

www.ingramcontent.com/pod-product-compliance
Lightning Source LLC
Chambersburg PA
CBHW061647040426
42446CB00010B/1615